marie claire

10 years of great food

with
michele cranston

marie claire

10 years of great food

with
michele cranston

MURDOCH BOOKS

contents

Introduction

I'm often asked what makes a '*marie claire*' cookbook and so, having just completed my 10th book in the series, I thought it was time to look back over the past 10 years and re-visit some old favourites.

I had been working in food media for only a year when I wrote my first *marie claire* cookbook, although I had been a cook for almost twenty years prior to that. I had escaped the professional kitchen and found myself in my own, working on my many ideas — what a joyful place to find oneself! Ten years on, I am still in my kitchen and still excited about food. In fact, even as I've been putting this book together I've been jotting down future ideas, expanding on recipes found in these pages, or letting memories of past food-adventures inspire me.

Over the years, during talks I have given about writing cookbooks, I have found people to be fascinated by how I come up with so many recipes. They have also been interested by how and why the food is styled in such a way, who tests the recipes and so on. Compiling my favourite recipes seemed to be a great way to address some of these queries — so you'll find my own personal notes on the recipes throughout the book. They are my way of explaining the inspiration for the recipe, why it's a favourite of mine and what memories it conjures up. I think this is important because food is so integral to our personal and cultural history. For me, that is the wonderful thing about food and why I always laugh when anyone queries how I could come up with yet another book of recipes.

The other wonderful thing about working on a book is it is such a collaborative experience. I may be working on the bones of it but there is an enormous team around me filling in the missing pieces and fleshing the whole project out. Editors and producers ensuring that the words are correct and everything is where it should be, home economists testing the recipes to ensure that what I cooked at home works for everyone, designers arranging it all into a beautiful whole and the studio team who take the amazing photographs for which these books are renowned.

I have to say I love the time we all spend in the studio. I started my adult life studying art and somehow became sidetracked into the kitchen. It's a combination that works because I think about the aesthetics of food. When I'm writing a recipe I imagine how it will look, how it will taste, what the main flavours, colours and textures are, way before I actually put pen to paper. So to be in a studio for several weeks or months working with a creative team of photographers, stylists and prep chefs is my idea of heaven.

The end result is a beautiful book, which is a testament to all the hard work of the previous twelve months.

Looking back, I realise that the *marie claire* books are all about light and vitality, seasonal produce and of course delicious food. So come with me on a journey to enjoy the lush greens of spring time, the summery alfresco table, the earthy tones of autumn or a wintery afternoon of comfort food and enjoy the fresh flavours of *marie claire* all over again.

Michele

SPRING

a new start

Spring for me is always a time to shake out the old cobwebs
and become reinvigorated about the day-to-day patterns of life.
As the air begins to feel sunnier and lighter and the layered weight
of winter is slowly discarded, it's wonderful to embrace the flavours
of the new season. If I were to break a day down into seasons, then
the early morning would be springtime, with its crisp, bright air
and so I've started this chapter with fresh and fruity breakfast and
brunch ideas. Some people swear by an ocean swim or a jog around
the park as the perfect way to start a day but I'll happily settle for
berries and yoghurt, the perfect egg or an indulgent muffin.

pancakes with maple-berry butter

SERVES 4

250 g (9 oz/2 cups) self-raising flour
2 heaped tablespoons light brown sugar
400 ml (14 fl oz) buttermilk
2 eggs, separated
1 teaspoon natural vanilla extract
1–2 tablespoons butter, for greasing
fresh berries, to serve

maple-berry butter
200 g (7 oz) unsalted butter, softened
3 tablespoons maple syrup
100 g (3½ oz/about ⅔ cup) dried cranberries

To make the maple-berry butter, put the butter, maple syrup and cranberries in a food processor or blender and chop until well combined. Spoon onto a sheet of baking paper or plastic wrap and roll up to form a log. Refrigerate until ready to use.

To make the pancakes, sift the flour and sugar into a bowl and make a well in the centre. Add the buttermilk, egg yolks and vanilla and stir to combine. In a separate bowl, whisk the egg whites until light and fluffy. Fold the egg whites into the buttermilk batter.

Heat a non-stick frying pan over medium heat and lightly grease with a little butter. Spoon the batter into the pan, in batches, to form pancakes that are 8–10 cm (3¼–4 inches) in diameter. Cook until golden brown underneath, then flip the pancakes over and cook for a further minute or two. Transfer to a warm plate. Repeat with the remaining mixture, adding more butter to the pan as you need it.

Pile the warm pancakes onto serving plates. Serve with slices of maple-berry butter and a scattering of berries.

Butter flavoured with maple syrup and finely chopped cranberries slowly melting over warm pancakes ... do I need to say any more?

I've always loved the exotic fragrance of vanilla and I get really excited when I see a jar of plump beans on a deli shelf, as I know just what the jar smells like inside. In this recipe I've combined the heady aroma of vanilla with the sweet tang of citrus for a refreshing compote.

spring smoothie

....

SERVES 2

250 ml (9 fl oz/1 cup) fresh orange juice
160 g (5¾ oz/1 cup) chopped fresh pineapple
1 banana
pulp of 2 passionfruit
4 mint leaves
4 ice cubes

Blend the ingredients until smooth and pour into two chilled glasses.

citrus compote

....

SERVES 4

3 limes
3 oranges
2 pink grapefruits
1 vanilla bean, finely chopped
1 teaspoon sugar
260 g (9¼ oz/1 cup) honey-flavoured yoghurt

Zest one of the limes and one of the oranges and place the zest in a medium-sized bowl. Peel the limes, oranges and grapefruits with a sharp knife. Cut the flesh into segments, or thinly slice, saving any juice, and place in the bowl. Add the vanilla bean, sugar and reserved juice and mix to combine. Serve with honey yoghurt.

cinnamon ricotta with nectarines and honey

SERVES 4

230 g (8 oz/1 cup) fresh ricotta cheese
260 g (9¼ oz/1 cup) Greek-style yoghurt
½ teaspoon ground cinnamon
4 ripe nectarines, quartered
2 tablespoons honey

Put the ricotta in a bowl and add half the yoghurt and the cinnamon. Stir until well combined, then add the remaining yoghurt, folding it through until it gives a slightly marbled effect.

Spoon into four small bowls, or dollop onto four serving plates, then add the nectarine quarters. Drizzle with honey and serve.

black sticky rice with fresh papaya

SERVES 4

200 g (7 oz/1 cup) black rice
4 tablespoons grated palm sugar (jaggery) or light brown sugar
1 teaspoon natural vanilla extract
125 ml (4 fl oz/½ cup) coconut milk, plus extra, to serve
fresh papaya, to serve

Soak the rice in plenty of cold water for 1 hour. Drain, rinse, then drain again. Place in a saucepan with 500 ml (17 fl oz/2 cups) water. Bring to the boil, stirring occasionally, then reduce the heat to low. Cover and simmer for 35 minutes.

Stir in the sugar, vanilla, coconut milk and a pinch of sea salt. Simmer over low heat, uncovered, for a further 10 minutes, then take the rice off the heat and allow to cool. Serve with slices of fresh papaya and a drizzle of coconut milk.

Years ago I was travelling through the Greek Islands and stumbled across an early market. In one corner was a man selling the most amazing yoghurt, which he scooped into small cups from a large wooden tub and then drizzled with honey. Across the way was an abundant fruit stall piled high with warm figs. This recipe is a little twist on one of the best breakfasts I've ever eaten.

This is my cheat's version of black sticky rice. Traditional recipes take hours so I apologise if I've offended you with my shortcuts. It is a favourite of many I know and lots of fun to make at home.

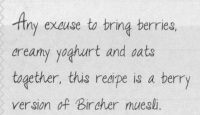

Any excuse to bring berries, creamy yoghurt and oats together, this recipe is a berry version of Bircher muesli.

I'm a big fan of muffins but they have to be hearty and healthy – not cakey or too sweet. I still like to think they are more breakfast than afternoon tea ...

berry breakfast trifle

SERVES 4

200 g (7 oz/2 cups) rolled
    (porridge) oats
250 ml (9 fl oz/1 cup) apple juice
500 g (1 lb 2 oz/3⅓ cups)
    strawberries, hulled
3 teaspoons honey
130 g (4½ oz/1 cup) plain yoghurt
155 g (5½ oz/1 cup) blueberries

Put the oats and apple juice in a bowl. Mix well, then cover with plastic wrap and refrigerate for at least 1 hour or overnight, to allow the oats to soak in the juice.

Mash half the strawberries with the honey, then mix them through the soaked oats along with the yoghurt. Slice the remaining strawberries.

Spoon half the oat mixture into four serving glasses, top with half each of the strawberries and blueberries, then cover with the remaining oat mixture and the remaining berries.

raspberry brown sugar muffins

MAKES 8

250 g (9 oz/2 cups) plain
    (all-purpose) flour
150 g (5½ oz/¾ cup, lightly
    packed) light brown sugar
½ teaspoon bicarbonate of soda
    (baking soda)
½ teaspoon salt
155 g (5½ oz/1¼ cups) frozen
    raspberries
80 ml (2½ fl oz/⅓ cup)
    vegetable oil
1 egg
200 ml (7 fl oz) buttermilk
1 teaspoon natural vanilla extract
70 g (2½ oz/⅓ cup) raw
    (demerara) sugar
½ teaspoon ground cinnamon

Preheat the oven to 180°C (350°F/Gas 4). Grease eight holes of a standard (60 ml/2 fl oz/¼ cup) muffin tin or line with paper cases.

Combine the flour, brown sugar, bicarbonate of soda and salt in a large bowl, then toss the raspberries through the dry ingredients.

In a separate bowl whisk together the oil, egg, buttermilk and vanilla. Pour the liquid ingredients over the dry ingredients and stir until they have just come together. Do not overmix.

Spoon the batter into the prepared muffin holes and top with the combined raw sugar and cinnamon. Bake for 20–25 minutes or until the muffins are cooked through. Remove from the tin and place the muffins on a wire rack to cool.

coconut muesli

SERVES 12 (MAKES ABOUT 1.2 kg / 2 lb 10 oz)

400 g (14 oz/4 cups) rolled (porridge) oats
145 g (5 oz/1 cup) unsalted sunflower seeds
2 tablespoons sesame seeds
125 g (4½ oz/1 cup) slivered almonds
130 g (4½ oz/2 cups) shredded coconut
250 ml (9 fl oz/1 cup) maple syrup
80 ml (2½ fl oz/⅓ cup) vegetable oil
40 g (1½ oz/¼ cup) thinly sliced dried peaches
35 g (1¼ oz/¼ cup) thinly sliced dried mango

Preheat the oven to 150°C (300°F/Gas 2). Put the oats in
a large bowl with the sunflower seeds, sesame seeds, almonds
and coconut and mix well.

Heat the maple syrup and oil in a small saucepan over low heat.
Pour this mixture, while still warm, over the muesli and stir so that all
the grains and seeds are well covered.

Spread the mixture over two baking trays and bake for 30 minutes,
stirring occasionally. Swap the trays around in the oven halfway through
baking. Remove from the oven and allow to cool.

Transfer to a large bowl, add the peach and mango and toss well.
The muesli can be stored in an airtight container for up to 1 month.

With lashings of coconut, dried peach and dried mango, this is a little bowl of morning sunshine that can be enjoyed any time of the year.

Okay, so I may not win brownie points with a dietitian for this one but, really, who could complain about starting the day with yoghurt, fresh berries and toasty, spicy, chocolate breadcrumbs?

chocolate and cinnamon breadcrumbs
with berries and yoghurt

SERVES 4

4 slices of stale sourdough bread, crusts removed
50 g (1¾ oz/½ cup) almond meal
1 tablespoon light brown sugar
1 tablespoon dark unsweetened cocoa powder
1 teaspoon ground cinnamon
1 tablespoon unsalted butter
250 g (9 oz/1⅔ cups) blueberries
250 g (9 oz/2 cups) raspberries
400 g (14 oz) plain or vanilla yoghurt

Preheat the oven to 160°C (315°F/Gas 2–3). Tear the bread into small pieces and place in a food processor with the almond meal, sugar, cocoa and cinnamon. Chop to form fine breadcrumbs, then add the butter and blend for a few more seconds.

Spread the chocolate crumbs on a baking tray and bake for 10 minutes, or until they feel crisp. Remove from the oven and allow to cool completely.

Arrange the berries and yoghurt in a bowl and sprinkle with the chocolate and cinnamon crumbs.

boiled egg and quinoa salad

SERVES 4

1 egg yolk
1 tablespoon lemon juice
125 ml (4 fl oz/½ cup) light olive oil
2 anchovy fillets, finely chopped
4 eggs, at room temperature
100 g (3½ oz/½ cup) quinoa
75 g (2½ oz/2¼ cups) wild rocket
  (arugula) leaves
1 tablespoon finely snipped chives

In a small bowl, whisk together the egg yolk and lemon juice, then slowly whisk in the olive oil to make a dressing. Whisk in the anchovies, then season to taste with sea salt and freshly ground black pepper.

Bring a saucepan of water to the boil and add the eggs. Boil for 5 minutes, then lift the eggs out of the water and leave to cool.

Put the quinoa in a saucepan and cover with 500 ml (17 fl oz/2 cups) water. Bring to the boil, then reduce the heat and simmer for 5–10 minutes, or until the grain is tender. Drain the quinoa, tip it into a bowl and stir through half the anchovy dressing.

Arrange a nest of rocket leaves on four plates, then spoon a pile of quinoa into the middle. Peel the eggs, slice them in half and sit them on the quinoa. Drizzle with the remaining dressing and sprinkle with the chives.

eggy toast with sweet chilli sauce

SERVES 4

4 thick slices of wholemeal (whole-
  wheat) bread, crusts removed
80 ml (2½ fl oz/⅓ cup) light
  olive oil
4 organic eggs
a handful coriander (cilantro) leaves
80 ml (2½ fl oz/⅓ cup) sweet
  chilli sauce

Using a cookie cutter, cut a circle from the centre of each of the bread slices. Discard the circles of bread.

Heat a large non-stick frying pan over medium heat and add the olive oil. When the oil is hot add the slices of bread and cook until just golden. Flip them over, then break an egg into the hole in each of the bread slices and cook for 1 minute. Reduce the heat to low and continue to cook for a few minutes, until the eggs are cooked to suit personal preference.

Serve with coriander leaves, a tablespoonful of sweet chilli sauce and freshly ground black pepper.

This is a high-protein start to the day. When I wrote this recipe seven years ago, quinoa was not well known and difficult to find, however it has now joined that 'superfood' section in most supermarkets.

Not that I'm admitting to the odd hangover, but if such a thing should happen, this is the perfect cure — fried, crunchy, eggy, spicy and sweet.

The feta cheese brings a lovely salty tang to these fritters. They are great by themselves but can also be served with smoked salmon or crispy bacon.

feta cheese and spinach fritters

MAKES 12

1 bunch (500 g/1 lb 2 oz) English spinach,
    trimmed and rinsed
3 eggs
155 g (5^1/2 oz/1^1/4 cups) self-raising flour
100 g (3^1/2 oz/^{2}/3 cup) crumbled feta cheese
4 spring onions (scallions), thinly sliced
^{1}/2 teaspoon freshly grated nutmeg
6 mint leaves, thinly sliced
2 tablespoons vegetable oil, for cooking
lemon wedges, to serve

Heat a large frying pan over medium heat. Put the spinach into the pan and cover with a lid. Cook for 3–4 minutes, turning occasionally, until the spinach is dark green. Remove from the heat and allow the spinach to cool. Remove any excess liquid from the spinach, then finely chop it.

Put the eggs and flour in a bowl and whisk to combine. Add the chopped spinach, feta cheese, spring onion, nutmeg and mint, and mix well. Season to taste with sea salt and freshly ground black pepper.

Heat a little of the oil in a frying pan over medium–high heat and drop heaped tablespoons of fritter mixture into the pan. Cook until golden brown on one side, then flip over and cook for a further 2 minutes. Remove to a warm tray and cook the remaining mixture, adding more oil as required.

Serve warm with wedges of lemon.

prosciutto with braised fennel and zucchini

....

SERVES 4 AS A SIDE DISH

2 fennel bulbs
3 tablespoons olive oil
juice of 1 lemon
2 zucchini (courgettes)
6 thin slices of prosciutto
10 mint leaves, torn

Preheat the oven to 200°C (400°F/Gas 6). Line a baking tray with baking paper.

Trim the fennel bulbs, reserving any feathery green fronds, and cut each bulb into eight wedges. Place them on the baking tray and drizzle with the olive oil and 1 tablespoon of the lemon juice. Season with sea salt and freshly ground black pepper, cover with foil and bake for 30 minutes. Remove from the oven and allow the fennel to cool a little, reserving the cooking juices.

Slice the zucchini into long, thin ribbons using a vegetable peeler. Tear the prosciutto into strips. Arrange the fennel, zucchini and prosciutto on a serving platter and scatter with the mint and reserved fennel fronds. Pour the reserved cooking juices from the fennel over the salad and drizzle with the remaining lemon juice.

These are a few of my favourite things – fennel, prosciutto and zucchini – thrown into a bowl. In winter I would cut both the vegetables into thick slices and roast them until lightly golden.

This is a fresh twist on the old classic of sardines on toast. I've used fresh ones but you could use tinned sardines instead (although there is no need to cook them). The tomato salad with its vinegary dressing lifts the richness of the fish.

The combination of avocado and bocconcini makes this a light and healthy lunchtime salad that's both filling and easy to prepare.

sardines on toast

SERVES 4

3 ripe tomatoes, finely diced
½ red onion, thinly sliced into rings
2 tablespoons white wine vinegar
2 tablespoons extra virgin olive oil
1 tablespoon oregano leaves
1 teaspoon butter
8 or 16 sardine fillets, depending on their
    size (300 g/10½ oz in total)
4 thick slices of wholemeal (whole-wheat)
    bread, toasted

Put the tomato, onion, vinegar, olive oil and oregano leaves in a small bowl. Stir to combine and season with sea salt and freshly ground black pepper.

Put a non-stick frying pan over high heat and add the butter. Cook the sardine fillets for 1–2 minutes on both sides, until they are opaque and slightly browned.

Pile the sardines onto the toast. Top with the tomato salad and any remaining dressing.

avocado, asparagus and bocconcini salad

SERVES 4

1 tablespoon white wine vinegar
80 ml (2½ fl oz/⅓ cup) extra virgin olive oil
20 mint leaves, coarsely chopped
a handful flat-leaf (Italian) parsley,
    coarsely chopped
350 g (12 oz/2 bunches) thin asparagus spears, trimmed
200 g (7 oz) bocconcini (fresh baby mozzarella
    cheese), cut in half
2 avocados

Put the vinegar, olive oil, mint and parsley in a large bowl.

Bring a saucepan of water to the boil. Add the asparagus spears and blanch for 1 minute, or until they begin to turn emerald green. Rinse the asparagus spears under cold running water, then cut them into 4 cm (1½ inch) lengths. Add them to the mint and parsley, along with the bocconcini.

Cut the avocados in half and remove the stones. Cut the flesh into bite-sized chunks or wedges and add them to the salad. Season with sea salt and freshly ground black pepper, then gently toss before serving.

sliced leg ham with a burghul salad

....

SERVES 4

10 bulb spring onions (scallions), trimmed
1 tablespoon balsamic vinegar
1 tablespoon olive oil
1 tablespoon caster (superfine) sugar
500 g (1 lb 2 oz) cherry tomatoes
90 g (3¼ oz/½ cup) burghul (bulgur)
1 teaspoon ground cumin
zest and juice of 1 lemon
2 tablespoons extra virgin olive oil
2 handfuls flat-leaf (Italian) parsley,
   coarsely chopped
8–12 slices of leg ham off the bone

Preheat the oven to 180°C (350°F/Gas 4). Cut the spring onions in half lengthways. Put them in a bowl with the vinegar, olive oil and sugar and toss until the onions are thoroughly coated. Spread them on a baking tray lined with foil and bake for 25 minutes, or until golden brown.

Add the cherry tomatoes to the baking tray and bake for a further 5–10 minutes, or until the skins are starting to split. Remove from the oven.

Put the burghul in a bowl, sprinkle over the cumin and cover with 125 ml (4 fl oz/½ cup) boiling water. Leave to sit for 10 minutes, to allow the grains to soak up the water.

Add the roasted onions and tomatoes, lemon zest, lemon juice, extra virgin olive oil and parsley. Season to taste with sea salt and freshly ground black pepper and toss to combine. Divide the ham among four plates and spoon the salad over the top.

Burghul brings that lovely cracked-wheat nuttiness to
tabouleh, so I thought it would be nice to toss it through
some stronger flavours. The tomato and ham work
surprisingly well with this crunchy grain.

With its soft-boiled eggs and crunchy vegetables, this is a great lunchtime or brunchtime salad. Ideally you'll have home-made egg mayonnaise on hand to dollop on top and some warm crusty bread to serve on the side.

High in protein and packed with leafy goodness, this salad is filling enough to serve at night. At lunchtime it will give you a super energy boost to see you through to the end of the day.

witlof and celery salad with boiled eggs

SERVES 4

4 organic eggs, at room
   temperature
2 witlof (chicory/Belgian endive),
   thinly sliced
2 celery stalks, thinly sliced
2 tablespoons finely chopped
   parsley
1 teaspoon cider vinegar
2 tablespoons extra virgin olive oil
2 tablespoons good-quality
   mayonnaise

Bring a saucepan of water to the boil and add the eggs. Boil for 5 minutes, then remove and allow to cool. Peel the eggs and cut them into big pieces.

Put the witlof, celery and egg in a serving bowl and sprinkle with the parsley.

Combine the vinegar and olive oil in a small bowl. Spoon over the salad, then add the mayonnaise in dollops.

tuna and quinoa salad

SERVES 4

150 g (5½ oz/¾ cup) quinoa
2 tablespoons lemon juice
2 tablespoons olive oil
1 tablespoon finely chopped
   preserved lemon rind
25 g (1 oz/1 bunch) chives, finely
   snipped
200 g (7 oz) green beans,
   blanched and cut into 3 cm
   (1¼ in) lengths, on the diagonal
250 g (9 oz) cherry tomatoes, cut
   into quarters
200 g (7 oz) tinned tuna in oil,
   drained and flaked
40 g (1½ oz/1 cup) mizuna
   or baby salad leaves

Put the quinoa in a saucepan and cover with 500 ml (17 fl oz/ 2 cups) of water. Bring to the boil, then reduce the heat and simmer for 5–10 minutes, or until the grain is tender. Drain and rinse under cold running water.

Put the lemon juice, olive oil, preserved lemon rind and chives in a bowl and add the quinoa. Toss together, then add the green beans, cherry tomatoes and tuna. Toss once more and season to taste with sea salt and freshly ground black pepper.

Divide the salad leaves among four bowls and spoon the tuna and quinoa salad over the top.

chicken with coconut sambal

SERVES 4

2 skinless chicken breast fillets,
  poached and shredded
3 tablespoons olive oil
1 tablespoon lime juice
100g (3½ oz/2¼ cups) baby
  English spinach leaves
1 large red papaya, sliced

coconut sambal

2 teaspoons vegetable oil
1 tablespoon finely chopped
  lemongrass, white part only
1 large red chilli, seeded and finely
  chopped
½ onion, finely diced
3 tablespoons desiccated coconut
1 teaspoon dark brown sugar
½ teaspoon sea salt

To make the coconut sambal, heat the oil in a frying pan over medium heat. Cook the lemongrass, chilli and onion, stirring, for 5 minutes. Reduce the heat to low and add the coconut, sugar and salt. Cook, stirring, for 5 minutes, or until the ingredients are golden and crisp. Remove from the heat and allow to cool.

Put the chicken, olive oil and lime juice in a bowl and toss to combine. Pile the spinach leaves on a serving platter. Arrange the papaya and chicken over the top, and sprinkle with the coconut sambal.

prosciutto and beetroot salad

SERVES 4 AS A STARTER

2 ripe roma (plum) tomatoes, diced
½ red onion, diced
1 Lebanese (short) cucumber, diced
1 tablespoon salted capers, rinsed
  and drained
1 teaspoon red wine vinegar
8 slices of prosciutto, cut in half
1 large beetroot (beet), peeled and
  grated
2 hard-boiled eggs, grated
2 tablespoons finely chopped
  flat-leaf (Italian) parsley
3 tablespoons extra virgin olive oil

Put the tomato, onion, cucumber, capers and vinegar in a bowl and toss together.

Arrange the prosciutto on a round serving platter and pile the beetroot in the middle. Spoon the tomato salad over the beetroot, then top with the egg. Sprinkle with the parsley, season with freshly ground black pepper and drizzle with the olive oil to serve.

It's the coconut sambal that brings this salad to life and reduces the sweetness of the fruit. If you're not fond of papaya you can substitute with mango, peach or rockmelon.

I've converted many a non-beetroot-eater with this salad. It may seem like a strange combination but the flavours work really well together. Easy to assemble and great to look at, this is definitely a fun one to share.

This wonderfully light salad can be served as a starter or a light meal. The fennel, parsley, mint and olives work beautifully with the rich flavour of the buttery squid.

squid and fennel salad

8 small squid tubes (about 750 g/1 lb 10 oz in total),
   cleaned (reserve the tentacles)
2 garlic cloves, crushed
½ teaspoon ground white pepper
3 tablespoons olive oil
3 tablespoons lemon juice
2 fennel bulbs, trimmed and thinly sliced
16 kalamata olives, pitted and coarsely chopped
a handful flat-leaf (Italian) parsley,
   coarsely chopped
1 tablespoon finely chopped mint
3 tablespoons unsalted butter

Rinse the squid under cold running water and pat dry with paper towel.
Cut the tubes along one side and open them out into a flat piece. Using
a sharp knife, lightly score the inside surface with crisscross lines — don't cut
too deeply, just enough to mark the flesh. Slice into 3 cm (1¼ inch) wide strips
and put the strips and tentacles in a non-metallic bowl. Add the garlic,
white pepper, olive oil and lemon juice, then toss well to coat. Cover and
refrigerate for 1 hour.

Put the fennel in a bowl with the olives, parsley and mint. Season lightly
with sea salt and freshly ground black pepper.

Drain the squid, reserving the marinating liquid. Heat 1 tablespoon of
the butter in a non-stick frying pan over medium heat and add the squid
a few pieces at a time. Cook for 2½ minutes on each side, or until the flesh is
opaque, then add the squid to the fennel mixture. Cook the remaining squid
in two more batches, adding more butter as needed.

When all the squid is cooked, add the marinating liquid and any remaining
butter to the pan and simmer over medium heat until the butter has melted.
Pour over the salad, toss well and serve.

smoked salmon with shaved vegetable salad

SERVES 4

1 fennel bulb, base trimmed, thinly shaved with a vegetable peeler
2 zucchini (courgettes), thinly shaved on the diagonal
    with a vegetable peeler
2 Lebanese (short) cucumbers, thinly shaved, on the diagonal,
    with a vegetable peeler
1 teaspoon finely chopped mint
1 teaspoon finely chopped dill
1 tablespoon olive oil
2 tablespoons lemon juice
1 teaspoon caster (superfine) sugar
½ teaspoon sea salt
16 slices of smoked salmon

Combine the fennel, zucchini and cucumber in a bowl with the mint, dill, olive oil, lemon juice, sugar and sea salt. Toss to combine, then set aside for 10 minutes.

Divide the smoked salmon slices among four plates. Toss the salad one more time before piling it on top of the salmon.

spicy prawn salad

SERVES 4

20 cooked prawns (shrimp), peeled and deveined, tails left intact
1 large red chilli, seeded and finely chopped
½ teaspoon cayenne pepper
½ teaspoon ground cumin
1 tablespoon finely grated fresh ginger
2 spring onions (scallions), thinly sliced
2 tablespoons lime juice
80 ml (2½ fl oz/⅓ cup) olive oil
a handful coriander (cilantro) leaves
2 small avocados, diced
couscous, prepared following packet directions, to serve

Put the prawns in a bowl with the chilli, cayenne pepper, cumin, ginger, spring onion, lime juice and olive oil. Toss to coat the prawns well, then add the coriander and avocado and season to taste. Lightly toss again and serve on a bed of couscous.

I love shaved vegetables in the warmer months and use my vegetable peeler with much gusto. Shaved fennel, zucchini, cucumber, asparagus, carrot ... the possibilities are endless.

This is a recipe for those of you who like a good chilli hit, so definitely not one to serve for friends with timid palates! The cayenne and cumin give the prawns a lovely, spicy heat, which the avocado and couscous will soften.

This is a salad that couldn't have been made in my childhood because in those days asparagus only came in a tin, parmesan was shaken out of a green tube and artichokes were unheard of. Thank goodness for the extensive range of foods now available!

asparagus and artichoke salad

....

SERVES 4 AS A STARTER

juice of 4 lemons
4 small globe artichokes
350 g (12 oz/2 bunches) asparagus spears, trimmed and cut in half
80 ml (2½ fl oz/⅓ cup) extra virgin olive oil
a handful (6 g/½ cup) flat-leaf (Italian) parsley leaves
50 g (1¾ oz) shaved parmesan cheese

Put the lemon juice in a large bowl, reserving 2 tablespoons for the dressing.

To prepare the artichokes, snap off and discard the leaves until you have reached the more delicate pale green ones. With a sharp knife, cut off the top half of each artichoke, cut it into quarters and drop into the bowl of lemon juice immediately, to prevent discolouration.

Using a sharp knife, remove and discard the furry choke from the centre, then thinly slice the quarters, returning them to the lemon juice and tossing them in it so they are well coated.

Bring a saucepan of salted water to the boil. Add the artichoke and lemon juice mixture and cook for 2 minutes. Add the asparagus and boil for a further minute.

Meanwhile, put the reserved 2 tablespoons of lemon juice in a large bowl with the olive oil. Season with sea salt and freshly ground black pepper and whisk to combine.

Drain the artichokes and asparagus then add to the bowl with the lemon vinaigrette. Toss to combine, then arrange on a serving platter. Scatter over the parsley and parmesan cheese.

grilled prawns with parsley and caper sauce

SERVES 4

1 tablespoon salted baby capers, lightly rinsed
a handful flat-leaf (Italian) parsley leaves
3 tablespoons lemon juice
155 g (5½ oz/¾ cup) wild rice
4 tablespoons butter
20 raw king prawns (shrimp), peeled and deveined, tails left intact
green salad, to serve

Combine the capers, parsley and lemon juice in a small bowl and set aside.

Bring a saucepan of salted water to the boil and add the rice. Cook for 30 minutes, or until tender. Drain and return to the warm saucepan.

Meanwhile, when the rice has 10 minutes remaining to cook, heat 1 tablespoon of the butter in a frying pan over medium heat and cook the prawns until pink and curled up (you may need to do this in several batches). Keep warm until ready to serve.

Melt the remaining butter in the pan. When starting to bubble, add the capers, parsley and lemon juice and swirl to combine.

Divide the rice between four plates, top with the prawns and drizzle the sauce over. Season with freshly ground black pepper and serve with a green salad on the side.

Every so often when writing recipes you hit upon a new combination that really excites the tastebuds. Brown butter and capers are a classic seafood accompaniment but the added nuttiness of wild rice definitely raises the flavour bar.

One of my favourite cuts of meat is the lamb backstrap. It's juicy, lean and lamby without being fatty — perfect for a serious sandwich like this.

marinated lamb and spinach
open sandwiches

SERVES 4

1 teaspoon thyme leaves
2 teaspoons sumac
1 teaspoon ground cumin
1 tablespoon sesame seeds
2 teaspoons lemon juice
2 tablespoons olive oil
2 lamb backstrap fillets
350 g (12 oz/1 bunch) English spinach, trimmed,
    well washed and drained
4 flat breads
110 g (3¾ oz/½ cup) hummus

Preheat the oven to 200°C (400°F/Gas 6).

Combine the thyme, sumac, cumin, sesame seeds, lemon juice and olive oil in a bowl and stir to combine. Add the lamb, toss to coat and allow to marinate for 10 minutes.

Heat a non-stick frying pan over medium–high heat and sear the lamb for a minute on both sides. Transfer the meat to a baking tray and put in the oven to cook for a further 5 minutes.

Meanwhile, add the spinach to the frying pan and cook for a few minutes, turning the leaves in the pan so they all wilt and turn dark green.

Season the lamb with sea salt, cover with foil and set aside for 5 minutes.

Warm the flat breads in the oven then put them onto four serving plates. Spread each flat bread with hummus, then top with the spinach. Cut the lamb into thick slices and divide evenly between the sandwiches. Serve immediately.

egg and cucumber salad

SERVES 4

4 fresh coriander (cilantro) roots, rinsed
    and finely chopped
1 large garlic clove, crushed
1 birds-eye chilli, thinly sliced
1 teaspoon light brown sugar
1 teaspoon sea salt
2 tablespoons lime juice
125 ml (4 fl oz/½ cup) olive oil
4 Lebanese (short) cucumbers, cut into chunks
½ red onion, finely diced
30 g (1 oz/1 cup) picked chervil leaves
30 g (1 oz/1 cup) picked coriander (cilantro) leaves
10 g (¼ oz/½ cup) picked mint leaves
10 chives, snipped
4 hard-boiled eggs, cut into large pieces
30 g (1 oz) pine nuts, toasted

To make the dressing, combine the coriander roots, garlic, chilli, sugar and sea salt. Add the lime juice and olive oil, whisk to combine and set aside.

Combine the cucumber, onion and herbs in a bowl. Pour the dressing over and toss gently to combine. Arrange the salad on a platter, top with the egg and scatter over the pine nuts.

How pretty is this salad? And it tastes as good as it looks. It's a simple idea with lots of crunch and a great sense of adventure.

There is something about fresh ricotta — I'm not sure if it's the softly plump texture or the intense milky flavour but I love using it in salads, especially with the often-overlooked butter lettuce.

butter lettuce, green pea and ricotta salad

SERVES 4

140 g (5 oz/1 cup) frozen green peas
100 g (3½ oz/1 cup) sugarsnap peas, trimmed
100 g (3½ oz/1 cup) snow peas (mangetout), trimmed
1 tablespoon lemon juice
2 tablespoons extra virgin olive oil
1 butter lettuce, rinsed and drained
230 g (8 oz/1 cup) fresh ricotta cheese

Bring a saucepan of salted water to the boil and cook the frozen peas
for 1 minute. Add the sugarsnap and snow peas and cook for a further
2–3 minutes, until they are emerald green. Drain, then rinse under cold
running water.

Put the peas in a bowl and add the lemon juice and olive oil. Toss and
season with sea salt and freshly ground black pepper.

Arrange the lettuce leaves in a serving bowl and spoon over the peas.
Add the ricotta in rough spoonfuls all over the salad.

mussels with rouille

SERVES 4

2 kg (4 lb 8 oz) mussels
2 tablespoons olive oil
1 white onion, finely chopped
2 garlic cloves, crushed
3 large ripe tomatoes, diced
1 bay leaf
1 fennel bulb, trimmed and thinly sliced
a pinch of saffron threads
1 teaspoon sea salt
250 ml (9 fl oz/1 cup) white wine
a handful flat-leaf (Italian) parsley leaves

rouille
1 thick slice of sourdough bread
a pinch of saffron threads
60 ml (2 fl oz/¼ cup) water
1 red capsicum (pepper), roasted and skinned
¼ teaspoon paprika
2 garlic cloves
125 ml (4 fl oz/½ cup) light olive oil

Clean the mussels in the sink under cold running water, scrubbing them to remove any barnacles or bits of hairy 'beard'. Throw away any that are open and that do not close when you tap them on the work surface.

Put the olive oil, onion and garlic into a large saucepan with a lid and cook them over low heat until the onion is translucent. Add the tomato, bay leaf, fennel, saffron and sea salt, and simmer for 10 minutes. Add the white wine, bring to the boil and tip in the mussels. Cover with the lid and cook for a few minutes, shaking the pan once or twice, then check that all the mussels have opened; throw away any that remain closed.

To make the rouille, tear the bread into pieces and put in a bowl. Bring the saffron threads to the boil in 3 tablespoons water in a small saucepan and then simmer for a minute. Pour the hot saffron water over the bread. Allow the bread to soak in the water and then add it to a food processor or blender with the capsicum, paprika and garlic. Blend until smooth, then add the olive oil in a stream to give a thick consistency. Season with salt to taste.

Divide the mussels between four big bowls, scatter over the parsley and serve with the rouille and crusty white bread.

Mussels always remind me of seaside holidays. This recipe is served with rouille – a wonderful Mediterranean mayonnaise flavoured with saffron and red capsicum. It's possible I was dreaming of the French Riviera when I wrote this recipe.

This is one of my picnic favourites. It's best to make it the day before, to let the flavours mingle and blend into the bread. What better way to greet the great outdoors than with thickly sliced pan bagna, chocolate brownies (see recipe on page 369) and a bowl of chilled grapes or cherries.

pan bagna

MAKES 6 PORTIONS

1 thin baguette
1 tablespoon extra virgin olive oil
1 garlic clove, peeled and cut in half lengthways
2 red capsicums (peppers), roasted, skinned and
seeds removed
1 tablespoon baby salted capers, rinsed and drained
185 g (6½ oz) tinned tuna, drained
15 black olives, pitted
½ small red onion, thinly sliced
15 basil leaves
a handful coarsely chopped flat-leaf
(Italian) parsley
10 anchovy fillets
100 g (3½ oz) marinated artichoke
hearts, drained

With a sharp bread knife, slice the baguette in half down its length and remove the bread filling from both the top and bottom portions. Brush the inside of the loaf with the olive oil and rub with the garlic.

Cut the capsicum into thin strips and combine with the remaining ingredients in a bowl. Season with sea salt and freshly ground black pepper and spoon insided the bottom half of the loaf, heaping it up. Reassemble the loaf, making sure that the sides meet neatly. Wrap in plastic wrap, place a weight on top (a bread board or heavy saucepan is suitable) and place in the refrigerator overnight. Slice into 6 portions and serve.

bloody mary

SERVES 1

150 g (5½ oz/¾ cup) finely chopped tomato
½ teaspoon salt
80 ml (2½ fl oz/⅓ cup) tomato juice
3 tablespoons vodka
1 teaspoon lime juice
1 teaspoon horseradish cream
¼ teaspoon worcestershire sauce
¼ teaspoon Tabasco sauce
a celery stalk and slice of lime, to serve

Put the tomato and salt in a bowl and allow to sit for 30 minutes.

Transfer the tomato to a blender, add the tomato juice and blend until smooth. Pour the blended tomato into a cocktail shaker with the vodka, lime juice, horseradish cream, worcestershire sauce and Tabasco sauce, and shake vigorously. Pour into a glass filled with ice and garnish with the celery, a lime slice and freshly ground black pepper.

rose petal sherbet sparkling water

SERVES 8

4 red organic roses, petals removed
220 g (7¾ oz/1 cup) sugar
1 tablespoon rosewater
2 litres (70 fl oz/8 cups) sparkling mineral water

Place the rose petals, sugar and 310 ml (10¾ fl oz /1¼ cups) water in a large saucepan and bring to the boil. Reduce the heat and simmer for 8 minutes, or until a light syrup has been made. Remove any scum as it forms. Cool and stir in the rosewater.

To serve, pour the syrup into chilled glasses and top with the sparkling mineral water.

In the distant BC (before children) days, Sunday mornings would often start with a Bloody Mary. Looking at this photo, I'm beginning to think it's a habit that should never have been broken.

This is a beautiful drink to serve at an afternoon tea when the girls have gathered around for a special celebration. Where possible, use homegrown or organic roses.

SPRING

light and luscious dinners

Springtime is all about new beginnings. Seasonally it is when the first green leaves are appearing, when young green vegetables like asparagus, beans, peas, broad beans and artichokes are at their best and when fresh herbs are abundant. The flavours of spring are fresh and lively with tangy citrus highlights and a sprinkle of Asian spices. Which is lucky because it's also that time, after the warming rich foods of winter, when we all start thinking about swimming costumes and bare summer skin, and begin making new resolutions to turn over a new leaf and eat light and healthy meals.

lobster salad with brown butter and capers

....

SERVES 4 AS A STARTER OR LIGHT MEAL

350 g (12 oz/2 bunches) asparagus spears, trimmed
45 g (1¾ oz/1 cup) baby English spinach leaves
2 cooked lobster tails, shells removed and flesh sliced
1 large red chilli, seeded and finely chopped
1 tablespoon small salted capers, rinsed and drained
2 tablespoons lemon juice
80 g (2¾ oz) butter

Blanch the asparagus spears in a saucepan of boiling water for 2 minutes, or until they turn emerald green. Drain and rinse under cold running water. Drain again. Divide the asparagus, spinach leaves and lobster among four serving bowls or plates.

Combine the chilli, capers and lemon juice in a small bowl. Put the butter in a small saucepan over high heat. When it begins to froth and turn brown, add the caper mixture and stir once. Remove from the heat.

Spoon the brown butter and capers over the salad and serve.

This is special-occasion food without the fuss, and whilst the flavours are rich they are not overwhelming. I've used cooked lobster tail but you could also make it with cooked crabmeat.

Because I nearly always have a small packet of 'just in case' smoked salmon in my refrigerator, it's so easy to turn out a simple meal like this that still feels a bit glamorous.

With its zingy Asian flavours and fresh crunch, this salad is a great accompaniment to seafood and chicken.

smoked salmon salad

SERVES 4 AS A STARTER

2 tablespoons olive oil
1 tablespoon lemon juice
a handful of flat-leaf (Italian) parsley
1 tablespoon small salted capers, rinsed and drained
1 fennel bulb, trimmed and shaved
8–12 slices of smoked salmon
1 avocado, thinly sliced
8 grissini

Put the olive oil, lemon juice, parsley, capers and fennel in a bowl. Season lightly with sea salt and freshly ground black pepper, and toss to combine.

Arrange the smoked salmon on four serving plates. Top with the avocado slices and the fennel salad, and serve with grissini.

asian-style vegetable salad

SERVES 6 AS A SIDE DISH

1 teaspoon sambal oelek
1 tablespoon finely chopped lemongrass
2 tablespoons lime juice
1 tablespoon grated palm sugar (jaggery)
1 tablespoon chopped mint
300 g (10½ oz) green beans, trimmed and cut in half
1 red capsicum (pepper), julienned
90 g (3¼ oz/1 cup) bean sprouts
1 Lebanese (short) cucumber, julienned
8 cm (3¼ inch) piece daikon radish (see Note),
    peeled and finely julienned
1 carrot, peeled and finely julienned
35 g (1¼ oz/¼ cup) finely chopped roasted peanuts

To make the dressing, put the sambal oelek, lemongrass, lime juice, palm sugar and mint in a small bowl and stir to combine.

Blanch the beans in boiling water until they are dark green, then drain and rinse under cold running water. Put them in a bowl with all the remaining ingredients, except the peanuts, and toss together. Pour over the dressing, toss the salad and allow to sit for 15 minutes before serving. Sprinkle over the peanuts and serve with seafood, chicken or any simple rice-based dish.

NOTE: *Diakon, also known as mooli, is a large white radish. Its flavour varies from mild to surprisingly spicy depending on the season and variety. It can be freshly grated into salads or slow-cooked in broths, and is available from most large supermarkets or Asian grocery stores. Select firm vegetables with unscarred skins.*

avocado and sumac salad

....

SERVES 4–6

80 ml (2½ fl oz/⅓ cup) extra virgin olive oil
1 tablespoon white wine vinegar
½ teaspoon honey
1 teaspoon dijon mustard
2 teaspoons sumac, plus extra, for sprinkling
1 telegraph (long) cucumber, peeled
4 small ripe tomatoes, quartered
1 avocado, diced
3 tablespoons oregano leaves
1 cos (romaine) lettuce, dark outer leaves removed

To make the dressing, whisk together the olive oil, vinegar, honey, mustard and sumac in a bowl.

To make the salad, cut the cucumber in half lengthways and scoop out the seeds with a teaspoon. Cut the cucumber thickly on the diagonal and put it in a large bowl with the tomato quarters, avocado and oregano leaves.

Cut the heart of the lettuce into thick strips and gently toss them through the salad along with the sumac dressing. Transfer to a serving bowl and sprinkle lightly with a little extra sumac.

Just a simple salad made from the refrigerator staples of lettuce, avocado, cucumber and tomato, with the sweet sumac dressing and fresh oregano leaves providing a surprising flavour boost.

A light and crunchy tropical salad with the classic flavourings of fish sauce, lime juice, chilli, lemongrass and mint. If you don't wish to use fresh crabmeat you could replace it with flaked smoked fish.

Just like the lemon risotto over the page, this dish is another midweek standby. I always ensure I have pasta, parmesan and capers in the kitchen and fresh herbs outside.

crab and green bean salad

SERVES 4

50 g (1¾ oz/⅓ cup) peanuts
2 tablespoons grated palm sugar (jaggery)
  or light brown sugar
2 tablespoons fish sauce
80 ml (2½ fl oz/⅓ cup) lime juice
2 spring onions (scallions), thinly sliced
2 large red chillies, seeded and thinly sliced
1 tablespoon finely chopped lemongrass, white part only
200 g (7 oz) green beans, trimmed, blanched and sliced on the diagonal
155 g (5½ oz/1⅓ cups) bean sprouts, trimmed
150 g (5½ oz/about 1 cup) fresh crabmeat
a handful coriander (cilantro) leaves
10 mint leaves, coarsely chopped

Put the peanuts in a small saucepan over medium heat and dry-fry them for
2–3 minutes, or until they turn golden brown. Allow them to cool a little, then
put them in a blender or food processor and pulse until they are finely chopped.
    Put the sugar, fish sauce and lime juice in a large bowl and stir until the
sugar has dissolved. Add all the remaining ingredients, including the peanuts.
Toss well and transfer to a serving bowl.

leek and lemon fettucine

SERVES 4

3 tablespoons olive oil
3 garlic cloves, crushed
1 tablespoon oregano leaves
3 large leeks, white part only, rinsed and thinly sliced
400 g (14 oz) fettucine
finely grated zest of 1 lemon
1 tablespoon small capers, rinsed and drained
70 g (2½ oz/½ cup) grated parmesan cheese, plus extra, for serving
15 g (½ oz/½ cup) coarsely chopped flat-leaf (Italian) parsley

Bring a large saucepan of water to the boil. Heat the oil in a large frying
pan over medium heat and cook the garlic, oregano and leek until the leek becomes
soft and translucent. Season with sea salt and freshly ground black pepper. Cook
the pasta in the boiling water until *al dente*, then drain and return it to the warm
pan. Add the leek mixture, lemon zest, capers, parmesan and parsley, and stir
through the pasta. Divide between four bowls and serve with extra parmesan.

lemon risotto with seared prawns

SERVES 4

1 litre (35 fl oz/4 cups) fish or vegetable stock
2 tablespoons butter
2 garlic cloves, finely chopped
2 leeks, white part only, rinsed and thinly sliced
finely grated zest and juice of 1 lemon
330 g (12 oz/1½ cups) risotto rice
4 tablespoons grated parmesan cheese
extra virgin olive oil
16 raw king prawns (shrimp), peeled and deveined, tails left intact
flat-leaf (Italian) parsley, to garnish

Bring the stock to the boil in a saucepan, then reduce the heat and keep at a low simmer.

Melt the butter in a large saucepan over medium heat. Add the garlic and leek and sauté for 5 minutes, or until the leek is soft and translucent. Add the lemon zest and rice and stir for 1 minute, or until the rice is well coated and the grains are glossy.

Ladle 250 ml (9 fl oz/1 cup) of the hot stock into the pan with the rice and simmer, stirring occasionally, until it has been completely absorbed. Add another 250 ml of the stock and cook, stirring, for another few minutes until it has been completely absorbed. Add another 250 ml of the stock and cook, stirring occasionally, until all of the liquid has been absorbed. Test the rice to see if it is *al dente*.

If the rice needs more cooking, stir in the remaining stock. When the rice is cooked, lightly fold through the parmesan and half of the lemon juice. Remove the pan from the heat while you cook the prawns.

Heat a little oil in a large frying pan over high heat and sear the prawns on both sides for 2–3 minutes, until they turn pink and begin to curl up. Pour the remaining lemon juice over the prawns, then remove from the heat.

Spoon the risotto into four warmed pasta bowls and top with the prawns. Serve drizzled with olive oil and scattered with parsley.

If you love citrus flavours, then lemon risotto is a great recipe to master for those times when it appears there is nothing for dinner. Most of the ingredients can be kept in the cupboard and a lemon is always lurking somewhere. Of course, if you've shopped in advance you can throw the golden prawns on top as well.

This is an Asian-style soup with citrus and chilli zing. Intensely flavoured, it's really a meal in a bowl so serve it with crusty bread. I always think fruit and sorbet (see pages 88, 91, 184 and 187) is the perfect dessert to follow.

tangy shellfish broth

8 raw king prawns (shrimp)
3 lemongrass stems
100 g (3½ oz) oyster mushrooms, cut in half
100 g (3½ oz) enoki mushrooms
6 kaffir lime leaves
3 roma (plum) tomatoes, finely chopped
2 spring onions (scallions), thinly sliced
juice of 3 limes
1 large red chilli, seeded and finely chopped
2–4 tablespoons fish sauce, or to taste
50 g (1¾ oz/½ cup) fresh crabmeat
a handful of coriander (cilantro) leaves,
    coarsely chopped
a handful of mint leaves

Peel and devein the prawns, reserving the shells. Cut off and reserve the pale ends of the lemongrass stems, then cut the long green stalks into 2 cm (3/4 inch) lengths and flatten them with a cleaver or the end of a heavy-handled knife.

Heat 1 litre (35 fl oz/4 cups) water in a saucepan. Add the prawn shells and the pale ends of the lemongrass and bring to the boil. Take the pan off the heat and strain the prawn stock into a large bowl to remove the solids.

Pour the prawn stock back into the saucepan, then add the crushed green lemongrass stems, mushrooms, lime leaves and tomato. Return to the boil, then reduce the heat and simmer for 3–4 minutes.

Add the prawns, and when they start to turn pink, add the spring onion, lime juice, chilli, fish sauce and crabmeat. Stir well, then season to taste.

Ladle into bowls and serve scattered with coriander and mint.

For those of you who love tongue-numbing sichuan peppercorns, this is a perfect springtime dinner — spicy pork with lots of orange, fennel and chervil to knock back the peppery heat.

sichuan pork with an orange fennel salad

SERVES 4

2 fennel bulbs, trimmed and thinly sliced
4 oranges, peeled and thinly sliced
2 teaspoons sea salt
2 teaspoons sichuan peppercorns
1 teaspoon white peppercorns
4 x 150 g (5½ oz) pork steaks, flattened schnitzel style
2 teaspoons olive oil, for frying
20 g (¾ oz/1 cups) picked chervil
80 ml (2½ fl oz/⅓ cup) extra virgin olive oil

Put the fennel and orange in a bowl with 1 teaspoon of the sea salt. Set aside.

Pulse the sichuan peppercorns, white peppercorns and the remaining teaspoon of sea salt in a spice grinder, or crush using a mortar and pestle. Pour the spice mixture onto a plate and press the pork steaks into it, coating each steak well.

Heat the olive oil in a non-stick frying pan over medium heat. When the oil begins to shimmer, put the steaks into the pan and cook for 4–5 minutes on each side. Remove from the heat, allow to rest for 5 minutes, then cut into thick slices.

Toss the chervil and extra virgin olive oil through the fennel and orange, and put a layer of the salad on four serving plates. Top with pork slices and repeat with the salad and pork slices to form two layers.

poached vegetables

2 tablespoons olive oil
2 garlic cloves, crushed
1 leek, white part only, rinsed and finely chopped
1 rosemary sprig
1 tablespoon thyme leaves
1 tablespoon finely chopped parsley
1 litre (35 fl oz/4 cups) vegetable stock
4 small pickling onions, peeled
335 g (11¾ oz/1 bunch) Dutch carrots, trimmed and peeled
350 g (12 oz/2 bunches) asparagus spears, trimmed
100 g (3½ oz) green beans, trimmed
100 g (3½ oz) zucchini (courgettes), cut into large chunks
100 g (3½ oz) baby (pattypan) squash, halved
couscous, extra virgin olive oil andva selection of condiments, to serve

Heat the olive oil in a large saucepan over medium heat and add the garlic and leek. Sauté for 2–3 minutes, or until the leek is soft. Add the herbs, stock and 500 ml (17 fl oz/2 cups) water. Bring to the boil, then reduce the heat so that the broth is just simmering. Add the onions and carrots and cook for 15 minutes, then add the remaining vegetables and cook for a further 7 minutes.

Remove the vegetables from the broth and put them on a warm serving platter. Pour the broth into a serving jug. Serve the vegetables and broth with couscous, extra virgin olive oil and a selection of condiments of your choice.

A fun dinner party recipe for vegetarian friends. The baby vegetables are all cooked in a lovely stock and served with couscous and your favourite accompaniments. I suggest harissa and salsa verde but you could also serve pesto, dukkah, green olive tapenade or chilli salt.

A delicious Asian twist on the classic roast chicken. In spring, serve with a green salad and in the cooler months, with steamed rice and Asian greens.

lemon and lime roast chicken

SERVES 6

2 kaffir lime leaves, sliced
1 lemongrass stem, white part only,
    trimmed and coarsely chopped
3 garlic cloves
2 cm (¾ inch) piece ginger,
    peeled and chopped
2 red chillies, seeded and chopped
2 tablespoons extra virgin olive oil
1 whole chicken
1 lemon, quartered
2 limes, quartered
2 long red chillies,
    halved lengthways

Preheat the oven to 180°C (350°F/Gas 4).

Put the lime leaves, lemongrass, garlic, ginger, chillies and olive oil into a food processor and blend to a paste.

Rinse the chicken under cold running water and pat dry with paper towel. Using your fingers, make a small pocket under the skin at the breast and insert half the seasoning paste. Rub the remaining paste inside the chicken and all over the skin. Arrange the lemons, limes and chillies on the base of a shallow roasting tin and sit the chicken on top. Cook for 1½ hours.

Remove from the oven, squeeze some of the hot lemon quarters over the chicken, then return to the oven for a further 5 minutes. Remove, cover with foil and allow to rest for 10 minutes. Carve into serving pieces and drizzle with the pan juices.

pan-fried bream with parsley salad

SERVES 4

a large handful flat-leaf (Italian) parsley, chopped
250 g (9 oz) cherry tomatoes, cut in half
25 g (1 oz/1 bunch) chives, snipped into 3 cm (1¼ inch) lengths
½ red onion, thinly sliced
2 tablespoons small salted capers, rinsed and drained
zest and juice of 1 lemon
2 tablespoons olive oil
100 g (3½ oz/scant ½ cup) fine semolina
1 tablespoon finely chopped dill
4 x 150 g (5½ oz) bream fillets
2½ tablespoons butter
lemon wedges, to serve

Preheat the oven to 180°C (350°F/Gas 4).

To make the parsley salad, put the parsley, cherry tomatoes, chives, onion, capers, lemon zest, lemon juice and olive oil in a bowl and toss well. Season with freshly ground black pepper and set aside.

Put the semolina and dill in a bowl and mix together well. Season with sea salt and freshly ground black pepper.

Rinse the bream under cold running water and pat dry with paper towel. Dip each fish fillet in the semolina mixture and gently press to coat well on both sides.

Heat the butter in a large frying pan over medium heat and fry the bream fillets for 2 minutes on each side, or until lightly golden. Now put them on a baking tray lined with foil and bake for 5 minutes, or until cooked through.

Serve with the parsley salad and lemon wedges.

One of my pet hates is ordering a piece of fish in a restaurant only to discover that the chef has done something terribly clever with it. As far as I'm concerned a fresh fish fillet only needs a bit of seasoning and a tasty accompaniment to be outstanding.

Pork fillet is a lovely lean cut, well suited to a not-too-rich midweek meal. In this recipe it is slow-cooked in its marinade of sweet soy and served with an Asian salad.

As I've said previously, when it comes to seafood, keep it simple. Lemony burnt butter with a hint of cumin and salt is all this lovely fresh piece of fish needs.

maple-baked pork fillet with an asian salad

SERVES 4

1 teaspoon soy sauce
80 ml (2½ fl oz/⅓ cup) maple
   syrup
1 garlic clove, chopped
1 teaspoon sesame oil
juice of 1 lime
2 x 200 g (7 oz) pork fillets
1 star anise
2 large red chillies, seeded
   and thinly sliced
100 g (3½ oz) snow peas
   (mangetout), trimmed and
   julienned
2 spring onions (scallions), thinly
   sliced on the diagonal
1 small daikon radish (see Note on
   page 53), peeled and julienned
1 red capsicum (pepper), julienned

Put the soy sauce, maple syrup, garlic, sesame oil and lime juice in a small non-metallic bowl and stir to combine. Put the pork fillets in a ceramic baking dish and cover with the marinade. Add the star anise and sliced chilli and cover with a lid or foil. Marinate overnight.

Preheat the oven to 150°C (300°F/Gas 2).

Remove the baking dish from the refrigerator and allow it to sit for 30 minutes, then bake the pork, covered, for 45 minutes.

To make the salad, put all the julienned vegetables in a bowl, reserving some of the capsicum for garnishing, and toss to combine.

Divide the salad among four plates or shallow bowls. Slice the cooked pork and arrange the slices on top of the salad. Drizzle with some of the sauce from the baking dish, scatter over the reserved capsicum and serve.

pan-fried bream with cumin and lemon salt

SERVES 4

1 teaspoon cumin seeds
1 tablespoon sea salt
juice and finely grated zest of
   1 lemon
4 x 180 g (6¼ oz) bream fillets
40 g (1½ oz) butter
leafy green salad, to serve

Heat a small frying pan over high heat and add the cumin seeds. Fry until they are aromatic and starting to darken, then remove them to a mortar. Add the sea salt and finely grated lemon zest, reserving a little, and grind the ingredients with a pestle until they are well combined. Set aside.

Rinse the fish fillets under cold running water and pat dry with paper towel. Heat a large frying pan over high heat and add the butter. When it is sizzling, put the fillets into the pan, skin side down, and cook for 5 minutes. Turn the fillets over, drizzle with the lemon juice and cook for a further 5 minutes, or until cooked through.

Serve the bream with a leafy green salad, a sprinkle of the flavoured salt and the reserved grated lemon zest.

minute steak with mushroom salad

SERVES 4

1 red onion, thinly sliced
1 tablespoon sea salt
1 tablespoon rosemary
2 garlic cloves, coarsely chopped
2 tablespoons olive oil
650 g (1 lb 7 oz) piece of beef
    sirloin, or 3 x 200 g (7 oz)
    sirloin steaks,
    cut into 12 thin slices
250 g (9 oz/2¾ cups) thinly sliced
    button mushrooms
3 tablespoons extra virgin olive oil
1 tablespoon red wine vinegar
250 g (9 oz) cherry tomatoes,
    halved
30 g (1 oz/¾ cup) baby rocket
    (arugula) leaves

Put the onion in a bowl with the sea salt. Toss to ensure the onion is well coated, then cover and set aside for 20 minutes.

Meanwhile, put the rosemary, garlic, olive oil and steak slices in a separate bowl and toss until the beef is well coated in the marinade. Toss the mushrooms in another bowl with the extra virgin olive oil and vinegar.

Put the onion in a sieve and lightly rinse under cold running water. Squeeze off any excess water, then add the onion to the mushrooms, along with the cherry tomatoes.

Heat a non-stick frying pan over high heat and cook the steak slices in batches for 1 minute on each side. As you finish cooking each piece of steak, allow it to rest on a warm plate until all the meat is cooked. Season to taste with sea salt and freshly ground black pepper.

Stack the steak slices on four warmed plates and drizzle with any remaining dressing or meat juices. Serve with some mushroom salad and rocket leaves.

chicken and preserved lemon salad

SERVES 4

1 tablespoon sea salt
juice of 2 lemons
2 skinless chicken breast fillets
3 tablespoons olive oil
1 teaspoon ground cumin
1 tablespoon finely chopped
    preserved lemon rind
95 g (3¼ oz/1 cup) flaked almonds,
    toasted
a handful coriander (cilantro)
    leaves, coarsely chopped
a handful mint, coarsely chopped
1 Lebanese (short) cucumber, diced
55 g (2 oz/⅓ cup) currants
couscous, prepared following
    packet directions, to serve

Bring a saucepan of water to the boil. Add the sea salt, half the lemon juice and the chicken breasts. When the liquid returns to the boil, cover with a tightly-fitting lid and remove from the heat. Allow to sit, covered, for 40 minutes — during this time the residual heat will gently poach the chicken.

Remove the chicken from the poaching liquid and coarsely shred it into a large bowl. Add the remaining lemon juice, olive oil, cumin, preserved lemon rind and flaked almonds. Toss together briefly, then add the remaining salad ingredients and toss again. Serve with couscous.

This is a quick and easy minute steak salad that takes minimum time to prepare, and can be cooked in a frying pan or on a barbecue. It is a light springtime twist on steak and mushrooms.

Salty and sweet, crunchy and fresh, the combination of currants, preserved lemon, almonds and cucumber is really seductive. You can also chop the salad ingredients finely and serve alongside a roast or barbecued chicken.

I love an oven-roasted tomato, all squishy, sweet, succulent and richly flavoured. In this recipe, think of the tomatoes as a chunky sauce rather than a separate ingredient.

seared lamb fillets with roasted tomatoes and chipotle chilli couscous

SERVES 4

16 large truss tomatoes
190 g (6¾ oz/1 cup) instant couscous
1 tablespoon butter
1 tablespoon finely chopped tinned chipotle chilli
1 Lebanese (short) cucumber, diced
a handful of coriander (cilantro) leaves
600 g (1 lb 5 oz) lamb loin fillets

Preheat the oven to 180°C (350°F/Gas 4). Cut the tomatoes in half and place on a baking tray. Season with a little sea salt and freshly ground black pepper and roast for 30 minutes.

Meanwhile, put the couscous, butter and chilli in a large bowl and pour 250 ml (9 fl oz/1 cup) boiling water over the top. Cover and allow to sit for 5 minutes, then fluff up the grains with a fork. Cover again and leave for a further 5 minutes. When the couscous has absorbed all the water, rub the grains with your fingertips to remove any lumps. When the couscous has cooled, add the cucumber and coriander.

Heat a large non-stick frying pan over high heat. Add the lamb fillets and sear for 2 minutes. Turn them over, reduce the heat to low and cook for a further 3–4 minutes. Transfer to a warm plate, cover with foil and allow to rest for 5 minutes.

Divide the couscous among four plates. Slice the lamb fillets on the diagonal and arrange over the couscous. Top with the baked tomatoes and drizzle with any meat juices.

steamed snapper with chilli caramel

SERVES 4

4 x 150 g (5½ oz) snapper fillets
200 g (7 oz) daikon radish (see Note on page 53),
    peeled and finely julienned
½ red capsicum (pepper), finely julienned
100 g (3½ oz) snow peas (mangetout), trimmed and
    finely julienned
4 lime cheeks, to serve

chilli caramel
2 red chillies, seeded and finely chopped
1 tablespoon finely chopped lemongrass white part only
1 tablespoon olive oil
1 tablespoon caster (superfine) sugar
2 tablespoons white wine vinegar
1 teaspoon soy sauce

To make the chilli caramel, sweat the chilli and lemongrass in the olive oil in
a small saucepan over low heat for 5 minutes. Add the sugar, vinegar and
1 tablespoon water, and cook until the mixture turns into a syrup. Remove from
the heat, add the soy sauce and allow to cool.

Fill a large wide saucepan with water to a depth of 6 cm (2½ inches) and
bring to the boil.

Rinse the fish under cold running water and pat dry with paper towel.

Rest the base of a bamboo steamer in the boiling water. Line a second
bamboo steaming basket with a square of baking paper, sit the fish fillets on
the paper and sprinkle with a little sea salt. Cover the basket, then sit it on top
of the bamboo steamer base and steam the fish for 7–8 minutes, depending on
the thickness of the fillets.

Meanwhile, toss the daikon, capsicum and snow peas in a large bowl.

Put the steamed fish on four warm serving plates and drizzle with the chilli
caramel. Serve with the salad and the lime cheeks.

The chilli caramel is a slightly more elegant version of good old Thai-style sweet chilli sauce. Delicious spooned over seafood or chicken, it's a handy condiment to have stored in a jar in the refrigerator.

Tropical fruits all start to appear in spring and this recipe uses everyone's favourites in the chutney made with mango and flavoured with ginger, lemongrass and tamarind. It's a delicious accompaniment to anything porky, from sausages through to a crispy roast.

roast pork with mango chutney

SERVES 6

1.5 kg (3 lb 5 oz) pork shoulder, skin scored
   (ask your butcher to do this)
green salad, to serve

mango chutney
1 tablespoon olive oil
1 red onion, finely diced
1 tablespoon finely grated fresh ginger
2 tablespoons finely chopped lemongrass white part only
2 tablespoons tamarind purée (see Note)
125 ml (4 fl oz/½ cup) white wine vinegar
115 g (4 oz/½ cup firmly packed) dark brown sugar
1 large red chilli, seeded and finely chopped
2 just-ripe mangoes, diced

To make the mango chutney, heat the olive oil in a saucepan over medium heat and add the onion, ginger and lemongrass. Cook, stirring, for 10–12 minutes, or until the onion is slightly caramelised. Stir in the remaining ingredients, bring to the boil, then reduce the heat and simmer for 20 minutes. Set aside.

Meanwhile, preheat the oven to 220°C (425°F/Gas 7). Pat the pork dry with paper towel and rub the scored skin with a generous amount of salt. Season with freshly ground black pepper.

Sit the pork in a roasting tin, skin side up, and roast for 25 minutes, then reduce the oven temperature down to 180°C (350°F/Gas 4) and cook for a further 1 hour. To test if the meat is done, insert a sharp knife or skewer into the centre — the juices should run clear.

Transfer the pork to a warm serving platter, then cover loosely with foil and leave to rest for 15 minutes. If the skin isn't quite crunchy and needs further cooking, slice it off using a sharp knife, put it back in the roasting tin and roast on the top shelf of the oven for a few minutes.

Carve the pork and serve with the mango chutney and a green salad.

NOTE: *Tamarind is the sour pulp of an Asian fruit. It is most commonly available compressed into cakes or refined as tamarind concentrate or purée in jars. Tamarind purée is widely available; the pulp can be found in Asian grocery stores.*

baked blue eye cod with herb salad

SERVES 4

1 tablespoon olive oil

8 spring onions (scallions), cut into 5 cm (2 inch)
    pieces and sliced lengthways

1 teaspoon dried chilli flakes

4 x 185 g (6½ oz) blue eye cod fillets

1½ teaspoons finely grated lemon zest

20 g (¾ oz) butter

3 tablespoons fresh orange juice

2 tablespoons walnut oil

1½ teaspoons lemon juice

30 g (1 oz/½ cup) dill, coarsely chopped

10 g (¼ oz/⅓ cup) flat-leaf (Italian) parsley leaves, coarsely chopped

10 g (¼ oz/⅓ cup) mint leaves, finely chopped

20 g (¾ oz/⅓ cup) chives, snipped

Preheat the oven to 200°C (400°F/Gas 6).

Heat the olive oil in a non-stick frying pan and cook the spring onion and chilli flakes until the spring onion is soft and beginning to colour.

Rinse the fish fillets under cold running water and pat dry with paper towel. Put the fish fillets into a roasting tin and cover with the cooked spring onions and lemon zest. Dot each piece of fish with the butter and pour the orange juice into the dish. Cover and bake in the oven for 15 minutes.

Put the walnut oil and lemon juice into a bowl and whisk to combine.

Put the fish onto four serving plates and spoon some of the juices over. Top with the mixed herbs and drizzle with the walnut and lemon dressing.

This is the perfect springtime meal – it's light, healthy and celebrates the best of the season. Fresh, sweet-fleshed fish, herbs by the handful and a buttery orange sauce.

I know it's a divided camp, but I for one have never been a ham-and-pineapple-pizza person. I just don't understand the tinned pineapple, cheese and dough combo. However, a succulent piece of roast pork with thinly sliced, tartly fresh pineapple is a different story.

roast pork with a pineapple glaze

SERVES 6 AS A STARTER OR LIGHT MEAL

500 ml (17 fl oz/2 cups) pineapple juice

3 tablespoons maple syrup

2 garlic cloves, finely chopped

4 star anise

2 cinnamon sticks

3 large red chillies, seeded and cut into large pieces

1 kg (2 lb 4 oz) pork loin, skin cut off and reserved

2 tablespoons balsamic vinegar

12 thin pineapple slices, skin and core removed

green salad, to serve

Make a marinade by mixing the pineapple juice and maple syrup together in a large non-metallic bowl with the garlic, star anise, cinnamon sticks and chilli. Using a sharp knife, cut 5 mm (1/4 inch) deep slashes into the pork, 4–5 cm (1½–2 inches) apart. Sit the pork in the marinade, roll it around until well coated, then cover and marinate in the refrigerator overnight.

Heat the oven to 200°C (400°F/Gas 6). Transfer the pork into a roasting tin, pour the marinade all over and around the pork, then cover with foil and roast for 40 minutes.

Meanwhile, make the crackling. Score the pork skin lightly using a very sharp knife, then cut it into several strips. Put the strips in a roasting tin, brush them with water, sprinkle with sea salt and roast for 20 minutes, or until golden brown and crackly. Drain off any fat.

Take the foil off the pork and baste the meat with the pan juices. Roast, uncovered, for a further 30–35 minutes, or until the juices run clear when a skewer is inserted into the thickest part of the meat. Remove from the oven, loosely cover with foil and allow to rest for 10 minutes. Meanwhile, stir the vinegar into the pan juices.

Carve the pork and serve on the pineapple slices with a spoonful of pan juices, a green salad and some bits of crackling.

soy-baked ocean trout

SERVES 4

4 x 200 g (7 oz) ocean trout fillets
1 tablespoon soy sauce
4 tablespoons Japanese rice seasoning (see Note)
300 g (10½ oz/20 spears) asparagus,
    trimmed and quartered lengthways
100 g (3½ oz) snow peas (mangetout),
    trimmed and julienned
1 red capsicum (pepper), julienned
1 teaspoon sesame oil
75 g (2½ oz/1 bunch) coriander (cilantro),
    rinsed and leaves picked
lime wedges, to serve

Preheat the oven to 180°C (350°F/Gas 4).

Rinse the fish fillets, pat them dry with paper towel and put them in a roasting tin. Drizzle with the soy sauce, then sprinkle with the Japanese rice seasoning. Cover the dish with foil and bake for 15 minutes.

Meanwhile, bring a saucepan of water to the boil. Blanch the asparagus and snow peas in the boiling water, then drain and refresh them under cold running water. Drain them again.

Put the asparagus and snow peas in a bowl with the capsicum and sesame oil. Toss to combine, then divide among four plates.

Arrange the ocean trout fillets on top of the julienned vegetables. Garnish with the coriander leaves and serve with lime wedges.

NOTE: *A traditional Asian condiment used to flavour rice. It is available from Asian grocery stores and from most large supermarkets.*

Traditionally used as a condiment, Japanese rice seasoning – or furikake – is a wonderful combination of seaweed, sesame seeds, dried fish, sugar and salt. Normally it's in my cupboard for sprinkling over plain rice or noodles but one day it occurred to me that the flavours would work really well with baked salmon.

My son will tell you that when it comes to lamb cutlets, my inner carnivore comes out. I just love nibbling on those bones! For this recipe, a little bit of thyme, lemon and olives is all you need.

The picture says it all ... yum. Grilled duck breast with a crispy sweet skin flavoured with quince paste. And all of that sugary richness is comlemented by the tangy bite of the grapefruit and watercress.

lemon and thyme lamb cutlets

SERVES 4

20 g (¾ oz/1 bunch) lemon thyme
12 lamb cutlets, French trimmed
3 tablespoons lemon juice
125 ml (4 fl oz/½ cup) olive oil
550 g (1 lb 4 oz) kipfler or salad potatoes
90 g (3 oz/¾ cup) pitted black olives
15 g (½ oz/½ cup) chopped flat-leaf (Italian) parsley

Put half of the lemon thyme into a glass or ceramic container and lay the lamb cutlets on top. Cover with the remaining thyme, the lemon juice and half of the olive oil, making sure the cutlets are well coated in the marinade. Leave to marinate for at least 1 hour or preferably overnight in the fridge.

Cut the potatoes into big chunks, put them in a large saucepan of salted cold water and bring to the boil over high heat. When the water has reached boiling point, cover the pan with a lid and remove it from the heat. Leave the potatoes to sit for 30 minutes.

Remove the cutlets from the marinade and barbecue or grill (broil) them for 2–3 minutes on each side, then allow them to rest.

Drain the potatoes and return them to the pan along with the olives, parsley and remaining olive oil. Stir vigorously so the potatoes are well coated and begin to break up a little. Season to taste.

Serve the cutlets with the warm smashed potatoes and a green salad.

quince-glazed duck breast

SERVES 4

4 boneless duck breasts, skin on
1 tablespoon quince paste
1 fennel bulb, trimmed and shaved or thinly sliced
2 handfuls (30g/1 oz/1 cup) picked watercress sprigs
2 pink grapefruit, peeled and divided into segments

Preheat the oven to 180°C (350°F/Gas 4). Score the duck skin in a crisscross pattern, then rub some sea salt into the skin. Heat a frying pan over high heat and sear the duck breasts, skin side down, until lightly browned.

Sit the duck breasts, skin side up, on a wire rack set over a baking tray. Put a teaspoon of quince paste on each duck breast and bake for 5 minutes. Take the tray out of the oven and spread the softened quince paste over the duck breasts. Bake for a further 10 minutes.

Meanwhile, put the fennel, watercress and grapefruit segments in a bowl. Season lightly with sea salt and freshly ground black pepper, then toss and divide among four plates. Thinly slice the duck breasts on the diagonal and serve with the salad.

pink grapefruit sorbet with morello cherries

SERVES 4

220 g (7¾ oz/1 cup) sugar
2 star anise
750 ml (26 fl oz/3 cups) fresh
    pink grapefruit juice
bottled morello cherries, to serve

Put the sugar, star anise and 250 ml (9 fl oz/1 cup) water in a saucepan over medium heat and bring to the boil. Stir until the sugar has dissolved, then remove from the heat.

Meanwhile, put the grapefruit juice in a large bowl. Pour the sugar syrup over the juice, remove the star anise and allow to cool at room temperature. Pour into a plastic container, cover with plastic wrap and freeze for 3 hours or overnight.

Remove the sorbet from the freezer and scoop into a food processor or blender. Blend to a smooth consistency, then return the mixture to the freezer until ready to serve.

Scoop the sorbet into four bowls and top with the morello cherries.

rosé jelly with raspberries

SERVES 4–6

400 ml (14 fl oz) rosé wine
2 teaspoons rosewater
150 g (5½ oz/⅔ cup) caster (superfine) sugar
1½ tablespoons powdered gelatine
raspberries and thin (pouring/whipping) cream, to serve

Heat the wine, rosewater and sugar in a small saucepan with 200 ml (7 fl oz) water over medium heat, stirring until the sugar has dissolved.

Pour 200 ml (7 fl oz) of the warm liquid, reserving the rest, into a small bowl and add the gelatine. Stir to dissolve, then return this liquid to the reserved liquid and stir through. Pour into a bowl, cover with plastic wrap and refrigerate for several hours or overnight, until set.

Layer the jelly in serving glasses with the raspberries and cream.

I always have a jar of morello cherries ready for a quick-fix dessert – spooned over ice cream, baked on a sheet of pastry or folded through a cake batter. Here I've given them a citrus kick with a mouth-tingling pink grapefruit sorbet.

I have to admit that I don't make real jellies often but whenever I do, I promise myself I shall make them more often. This is a childhood dream – jelly, cream and raspberries made just a little bit grown-up with a hint of rosé.

It does take a little time and patience, but home-made sorbet is delicious, especially with the wonderfully exotic flavours of pear and jasmine tea. This one is perfect to follow a meal of rich Asian flavours.

pear and jasmine tea sorbet

....

SERVES 4

3 tablespoons lemon juice
4 ya or nashi pears
375 ml (13 fl oz/1½ cups) jasmine tea, made using
   1 heaped tablespoon of tea leaves
80 g (2¾ oz/⅓ cup) caster (superfine) sugar
fresh longans or lychees, to serve

Pour the lemon juice into a non-metallic bowl. Peel and chop the pears, adding them to the lemon juice as you go so they don't discolour.

Put the pears, jasmine tea, sugar and 2 tablespoons of the lemon juice from the pears in a saucepan over medium heat. Simmer for 15 minutes, or until the pears have become opaque and soft. Set aside to cool.

Blend the pears and juice to a fine purée in a food processor or blender, then pour through a fine sieve into a plastic container. Allow to cool, then cover and freeze for 3 hours or overnight.

Remove the sorbet from the freezer and blend in a food processor to a smooth consistency. Return to the container and put into the freezer until ready to serve.

Serve scooped into bowls with the longans or lychees.

citrus curd

MAKES APPROXIMATELY 250 G (9 OZ/1 CUP)

2 large lemons
1 mandarin
100 g (3½ oz) unsalted butter
165 g (6¾ oz/¾ cup) sugar
3 egg yolks, whisked

Finely grate the zest of both lemons and the mandarin, then juice the flesh and pass the liquid through a sieve. You should end up with 170 ml (5½ fl oz/⅔ cup) citrus juice.

Pour the juice into a heavy-based saucepan and add the butter, sugar and grated citrus zest. Stir constantly over medium heat until the sugar has dissolved. Remove the pan from the heat and whisk in the egg yolks. Return to the heat and lightly whisk until the curd has begun to thicken, being careful not to let it come to the boil.

Pour the hot curd into a 300 ml (10½ fl oz) sterilised jar (see Note) and allow to cool. Seal with a lid and refrigerate until ready to use, the curd will keep for several weeks. Serve with warm brioche or toasted sourdough bread, or spoon over a sponge cake or into tartlet cases and top with whipped cream.

NOTE: *The best way to sterilise jars is to preheat the oven to 120°C (250°F/Gas ½). Wash the jars in hot, soapy water and then rinse well. Put the jars on a baking tray and place them in the oven for 20 minutes, they must be completely dry in the oven before using them.*

coconut pavlova with banana and passionfruit

SERVES 6

4 egg whites
150 g (5½ oz/1¼ cups) icing
   (confectioners') sugar, sifted
1 teaspoon white wine vinegar
1 teaspoon natural vanilla extract
25 g (1 oz/¼ cup) desiccated
   coconut
300 ml (10½ fl oz) thin (pouring/
   whipping) cream, whipped
3 bananas, sliced
pulp of 6 passionfruit

Preheat the oven to 150°C (300°F/Gas 2). Line a baking tray with baking paper. Using electric beaters, beat the egg whites with a pinch of salt until soft peaks form. Gradually beat in the icing sugar until the meringue is stiff and glossy. Fold in the vinegar, vanilla and coconut.

Spoon the meringue onto the baking paper to form a 20 cm (8 inch) circle. Using a spoon, make a slight dip in the centre and pull the edges up into soft peaks. Bake for 40 minutes, then reduce the oven temperature to 120°C (235°F/Gas ½) and cook for a further 30 minutes. Turn the oven off and allow the pavlova to completely cool in the oven with the door slightly ajar. Store in an airtight container until ready to serve.

Transfer the meringue to a serving plate. Pile the whipped cream in the middle of the pavlova and top with the banana and passionfruit.

My grandmother and great-aunts all made lemon curd and as a result there was always a hand-labelled jar of it in the refrigerator when I was young. It was spooned into tarts, dolloped onto warm scones and, my all-time favourite, spread over buttery wholemeal toast.

The great Antipodean pavlova is one of my favourite desserts. This one with its ripe bananas and passionfruit was a Cranston family classic.

SUMMER

the alfresco table

For me summer is all about the big outdoor table and all the
casual social get togethers that this implies. Friends gathered
for a long lunch under blue skies or spur of the moment
gatherings by the sea or under a shady tree. Food in summer
should be casual and easy to mark the indolent energy of
hot summer days and to be fair to the cook who would like
to be enjoying the languid days as much as everyone else.
I'm thinking smoky barbecues, shared platters of tantalising
flavours, easy and generous salads, chilled drinks and simple
fruity desserts.

Whenever we would go to my grandparents' house for Sunday roast, there would always be a plate of crisp vegetables for the children to munch on beforehand. It's a tradition that's been carried through the generations and I always serve a simple 'picky plate' for the children when entertaining. This, however, is a slightly adult version.

spiced crudités with a tarator sauce

SERVES 4–6 AS AN ENTREE

1 bunch baby carrots, trimmed and peeled
1 bunch radishes, trimmed
1 fennel bulb, trimmed and cut into strips
2 celery stalks, trimmed and cut into sticks,
    reserving the leafy ends
2 Lebanese (short) cucumbers, cut into strips
1 tablespoon sumac
½ teaspoon red chilli flakes

tarator sauce
2 slices of sourdough bread, crusts removed
60 g (2¼ oz) pine nuts, lightly toasted
1 garlic clove
80 ml (2½ fl oz/⅓ cup) lemon juice
3 tablespoons olive oil

To make the tarator sauce, soak the bread in cold water and squeeze it dry. Put the bread, pine nuts, garlic, lemon juice and olive oil in a food processor and whiz to form a smooth paste, then add water (about 2 tablespoons) to get the desired consistency for a dipping sauce. Transfer to a serving bowl.

Arrange the vegetables on a serving platter and sprinkle with the sumac and chilli flakes. Serve with the tarator sauce.

Italian white bean and tuna dip

SERVES 4–6

400 g (14 oz) tinned cannellini
  (white) beans,
  drained and rinsed
3 tablespoons extra virgin olive oil,
  plus extra, for drizzling
1 tablespoon lemon juice
95 g (3¼ oz) tinned tuna in oil,
  drained
a handful flat-leaf (Italian) parsley,
  chopped
8 kalamata olives, pitted and finely
  chopped
pide (Turkish/flat bread), toasted,
  to serve

Place the cannellini beans, olive oil, lemon juice and tuna in a food processor and pulse several times, to break up the beans but not mash them. Transfer to a serving bowl and fold through the parsley and olives. Drizzle with a little extra olive oil. Serve with toasted pide fingers.

eggplant dip with pomegranate seeds

SERVES 4–6

2 tablespoons olive oil
1 garlic bulb
1 large eggplant (aubergine)
90 g (3¼ oz/⅓ cup) tahini
  (see Note)
3 tablespoons lemon juice
sea salt to taste
a handful flat-leaf (Italian) parsley,
  chopped
1 teaspoon sumac
seeds from 1 pomegranate
sliced baguette or crispbread,
  to serve

Preheat the oven to 220°C (425°F/Gas 7).

Put the olive oil into a small baking dish. Using a sharp knife, halve the bulb of garlic from side to side, to cut the cloves in half. Put the garlic bulb halves cut side down into the dish and add the whole eggplant. Bake for 20 minutes, or until the garlic is golden brown and the eggplant is soft to the touch. Remove from the oven and allow to cool.

With the tip of a small sharp knife, remove the baked cloves from the garlic bulb and put them in a blender or food processor. Cut the eggplant in half, scoop out the soft flesh and add to the garlic. Blend, then transfer the mixture to a bowl and fold in the tahini. Add the lemon juice and salt, a little at a time, adjusting according to taste.

Just before serving, fold the parsley through the dip, sprinkle with the sumac and scatter over the pomegranate seeds. Serve with sliced baguette or crispbread.

NOTE: *Tahini is a thick, creamy paste made from husked and ground white sesame seeds. It is used to give a strong nutty flavour. Tahini is available in jars from health food stores and most supermarkets.*

As long as you have olives in the fridge and tinned white beans in the cupboard you can whip up this dip for any unexpected guests.

I love pomegranates. Richly coloured, sensually formed and totally impractical. However, here's a tip. Cut them in half, put them in a sealable plastic bag and smack the skin with a wooden spoon. The seeds should pop out, making them easy to scatter over this smoky dip.

I love the texture of freshly grated coconut - a little bit crunchy, a little bit milky — and so I thought it would be lovely to mix it with chilli and mint, and spoon it over freshly grilled prawns.

While this quick spicy rice is perfectly suited to both seafood and chicken, it really comes into its own when served with a vegetable curry or grilled vegetables topped with harissa.

grilled prawns with a fresh coconut salsa

SERVES 4 AS A STARTER OR LIGHT MEAL

2 tablespoons lime juice
1 garlic clove, crushed
2 tablespoons olive oil
24 raw king prawns (shrimp), peeled and deveined, tails left intact
100 g (3½ oz) piece fresh coconut, finely grated
1 large red chilli, seeded and finely chopped
8 mint leaves, thinly sliced
80 ml (2½ fl oz/⅓ cup) coconut cream

Put the lime juice, garlic and olive oil in a large bowl and stir to combine. Add the prawns and work the marinade into them. Allow to marinate for at least 10 minutes.

Combine the coconut and chilli in a bowl.

Heat a large frying pan over high heat and cook the prawns for 1–2 minutes each side, a few at a time, until they are pink and have curled up. Arrange on a serving platter.

Cook the coconut and chilli in the pan with the remaining marinade juices, then spoon over the prawns. Add the mint and a drizzle of coconut cream to serve.

spicy rice with nutty flavours

SERVES 4 AS A SIDE DISH

2 tablespoons olive oil
1 teaspoon cumin seeds
1 tablespoon sesame seeds
200 g (7 oz/1 cup) basmati rice
a handful (6 g/½ cup) of coriander (cilantro) leaves, coarsely chopped

Heat the olive oil in a large saucepan over medium heat. Add the cumin and sesame seeds and cook for 1 minute, or until the sesame seeds turn golden brown. Add the rice and stir for 1 minute. Pour in 500 ml (17 fl oz/2 cups) water and bring to the boil, stirring occasionally. Cover, reduce the heat to low and simmer for 15 minutes, or until the rice is fluffy and cooked through.

Quickly stir in the coriander and serve.

zucchini, tomato and bocconcini salad

SERVES 4

4 zucchini (courgettes)
1 teaspoon sea salt
2 ripe tomatoes, finely chopped
8 baby bocconcini (fresh baby mozzarella), halved
80 ml (2½ fl oz/⅓ cup) olive oil
1 tablespoon apple cider vinegar
2 basil leaves, thinly sliced

Create zucchini ribbons using a vegetable peeler. Put these in a bowl, sprinkle with the sea salt and toss several times to ensure the zucchini is well coated. Set aside for 10 minutes.

Drain any liquid from the zucchini and pat dry on paper towel. Arrange the zucchini ribbons on a serving platter. Top with the tomato and bocconcini.

In a small bowl, whisk together the olive oil and vinegar. Spoon this dressing over the salad and scatter over the basil. Season with freshly ground black pepper and serve with crusty bread.

Zucchini and tomatoes are in abundance during the summer months and this is a wonderful way to serve them in a salad. Salting the zucchini softens the flesh and intensifies the flavour.

This image says it all: friends, shared plates, quirky table setting and yummy food. During the photo shoot, this shot made us all hungry. The meatball sitting in the tahini was in my mouth before we had cleared the table!

chicken meatballs

SERVES 4

500 g (1 lb 2 oz) minced (ground) chicken
4 spring onions (scallions), thinly sliced
25 g (1 oz/½ cup) chopped coriander (cilantro) leaves
1½ teaspoons sea salt
1½ tablespoons sesame seeds
1 teaspoon dried chilli flakes
finely grated zest of 3 oranges
¾ teaspoon ground white pepper
mixed leaf salad, to serve

tahini dressing
135 g (4¾ oz/½ cup) tahini (see Note on page 98)
1 tablespoon lemon juice
sea salt and ground white pepper

Preheat the oven to 180°C (350°F/Gas 4). Line a baking tray with baking paper.

Put the chicken, spring onion, coriander and 1 teaspoon of the sea salt into a bowl and combine well.

Put the sesame seeds, chilli flakes, orange zest, white pepper and remaining sea salt into a large pasta bowl and stir to combine. Roll the chicken mixture into walnut-sized balls, roll them in the spice mixture and put them onto the prepared tray. Bake in the oven for 20–25 minutes, or until cooked through and golden brown.

To make the tahini dressing, put the tahini in a bowl and add the lemon juice. Stir several times, then add 80 ml (2½ fl oz/⅓ cup) water and continue to stir until smooth. Season to taste with sea salt and ground white pepper.

Serve the meatballs with a mixed leaf salad and the tahini dressing.

wilted spinach salad

....

SERVES 4 AS A SIDE DISH

1 kg (2 lb 4 oz/2 bunches) English spinach, stalks removed,
   rinsed, well drained and coarsely chopped
12 kalamata olives, pitted and coarsely chopped
1 garlic clove, finely chopped
2 tablespoons finely chopped mint
1 small red onion, halved and thinly sliced
2 tablespoons red wine vinegar
200 g (7 oz) feta cheese, crumbled
125 ml (4 fl oz/½ cup) olive oil
30 g (1 oz/1 cup) croutons

Put the spinach into a large metal bowl. Add the olives, garlic, mint, onion and vinegar, then scatter over the feta cheese.

Heat the olive oil in a frying pan over high heat until it is almost smoking, then pour it over the salad. Be careful to stand well back as some of the oil may splatter. Toss the ingredients quickly and pile them into a serving bowl. Scatter over the croutons and serve immediately.

A wonderful salad to serve for a shared feast, this recipe also provides a bit of fun and excitement in the kitchen when the hot oil is poured over.

Always a great way to use up leftover roast or barbecued chicken, this salad is special because of the sweet-spicy dressing with lots of wonderful Asian flavours. It would be equally as yummy spooned over freshly barbecued seafood.

This is my twist on the classic watermelon and feta salad. The onions are pickled in salt, which turns them a gorgeous hot pink and brings the required briny note to the sweet watermelon. As a salad it is delicious, unusual and very refreshing.

chicken and papaya salad

SERVES 4

2 tablespoons tamarind puree
   (see Note on page 79)
1 teaspoon soy sauce
2 teaspoons finely grated fresh ginger
1 tablespoon grated palm sugar
   (jaggery)
½ teaspoon ground cumin
1 large red chilli, seeded and thinly sliced
2 skinless chicken breast fillets, roasted
   and coarsely shredded
70 g (2½ oz/½ cup) peanuts,
   coarsely chopped
1 orange papaya, seeded, peeled
   and sliced
1 Lebanese (small) cucumber, diced
2 tablespoons Asian fried shallots
   (see Note)
2 spring onions (scallions), shredded
20 g (¾ oz/1 cup) mint leaves
15 betel leaves (see Note)

Mix the tamarind, soy sauce, ginger, palm sugar, cumin and chilli together in a large bowl with 125 ml (4 fl oz/½ cup) water. Keep stirring until the sugar has dissolved. Add the chicken to the dressing and toss it all together.

Combine the peanuts, papaya, cucumber, Asian fried shallots, spring onion and mint leaves in another bowl and season with sea salt and freshly ground black pepper.

To serve, arrange the betel leaves on four plates and top with the salad.

NOTE: *Asian fried shallots are available from the Asian section of any large supermarket. The shallots are made from fried red eschallots and are commonly used to flavour rice, soups and salads. Betel leaves are available from specialty Thai shops and make a great base or a leafy addition to any salad.*

watermelon salad

SERVES 4 AS A SIDE DISH

1 red onion
1 tablespoon sea salt
1 teaspoon caster (superfine) sugar
juice of 1 lemon
1 kg (2 lb 4 oz) seedless watermelon,
   cut into 2 cm (¾ inch)
1 Lebanese (short) cucumber, diced
2 teaspoons sumac
10 mint leaves, roughly torn
lime halves, to serve

Peel the onion, cut it in half and thinly slice it into half moons. Put the onion in a bowl and add the sea salt. Toss several times to ensure the onion is well coated, then cover and set aside for 30 minutes.

Drain the onion, then rinse under cold running water and squeeze out any excess liquid. Put the onion in a clean bowl and add the sugar and lemon juice. Stir to combine, then set aside for a further 30 minutes.

Remove the rind from the watermelon and cut the flesh into 2 cm (¾ inch) chunks. Arrange the watermelon and cucumber on a serving platter, sprinkle with the sumac and scatter over the mint leaves. Top with the pickled onion and serve with lime halves.

spiced feta salad

SERVES 4–6

125 ml (4 fl oz/½ cup) olive oil
2 garlic cloves, crushed
2 red chillies, seeded and finely chopped
juice of 2 lemons
1 teaspoon dried oregano
1 baby cos lettuce, thinly sliced
a handful flat-leaf (Italian) parsley,
     coarsely chopped
10 mint leaves, thinly sliced
1 red capsicum (pepper), finely diced
500 g (1 lb 2 oz) cherry tomatoes, halved
200 g (7 oz) creamy feta cheese,
     cut into small cubes
150 g (5½ oz) small black olives

To make the dressing, combine the olive oil, garlic, chilli, lemon juice and oregano in a small bowl.

Put the lettuce, parsley and mint into a large serving bowl and toss to combine. Top with the capsicum and tomato halves, and scatter over the feta cheese and olives. Drizzle with the dressing and serve.

This is a Greek salad with a bit of extra oomph. The garlicky chilli dressing works well with the capsicum and tomato, and brings a flavour burst to the creamy feta.

Micro herbs – or baby herbs/greens, as they're also called – have appeared in our supermarkets in recent years, and this is a perfect way to use them. Cut the tomatoes nice and thick to carry the lacy pattern that the green herbs create.

fresh tomato salad

SERVES 4

4 large ripe tomatoes, thickly sliced
a handful mixed fresh herb leaves
1 red onion, finely diced
2 large red chillies, seeded and finely chopped
3 tablespoons extra virgin olive oil
1 tablespoon balsamic vinegar

Arrange the tomato on a serving platter. Scatter with the herb leaves, onion and chillies. Season with sea salt and freshly ground black pepper.

Put the olive oil and vinegar in a small bowl and whisk to combine. Drizzle the dressing over the salad.

carpaccio of three fish

....

150 g (5½ oz) piece of sashimi-grade tuna,
   skin and bones removed
150 g (5½ oz) piece of sashimi-grade ocean trout,
   skin and bones removed
150 g (5½ oz) piece of sashimi-grade trevally or snapper,
   skin and bones removed
20 g (¾ oz/½ cup) mixed leaves
1 tablespoon lemon juice
2 tablespoons sesame oil
½ teaspoon sea salt
2 teaspoons lightly toasted sesame seeds, to serve
lemon wedges, to serve

Wrap each fish portion in plastic wrap and put them in the freezer for 30 minutes. Remove from the freezer and discard the plastic wrap and, using a very sharp knife, cut the fish into paper-thin slices. Arrange the slices on four serving plates.

Put the mixed leaves in a bowl and toss the lemon juice through. Pile the rocket onto the fish, drizzle with 1 tablespoon of the sesame oil and sprinkle with the sea salt. Combine the remaining sesame oil and the sesame seeds in a small bowl and serve on the side, to drizzle over individual serves, and serve with lemon wedges and a scattering of the mixed leaves.

A sashimi plate to share. The sesame oil dressing adds a lovely richness to the clean flavours of the raw fish.

Every so often I come up with a recipe to the soundtrack of Julie Andrews singing, 'These are a few of my favourite things!' No brown paper parcels tied up with string but prawns, chicken, chilli and lime.

This is an elegantly simple salad version of the classic rockmelon and prosciutto combination. However I've swapped the rockmelon for papaya, added orange juice for extra sweet juiciness and scattered over fresh basil leaves for extra flavour.

prawn and chicken salad

1 teaspoon ground cumin
2 teaspoons fish sauce
80 ml (2½ fl oz/⅓ cup) lime juice
80 ml (2½ fl oz/⅓ cup) olive oil
1 tablespoon sesame oil
15 mint leaves, thinly sliced
1 teaspoon sugar
350 g (12 oz) small cooked
    prawns (shrimp), peeled and
    deveined, tails removed
2 cooked skinless chicken breast
    fillets, shredded
1 carrot, grated
100 g (3½ oz) snow pea
    (mangetout) sprouts
1 telegraph (long) cucumber,
    peeled, seeded and diced
2 spring onions (scallions),
    thinly sliced
1 baby cos (romaine) lettuce,
    thinly sliced
2 tablespoons toasted
    sesame seeds

To make the dressing, combine the cumin, fish sauce, lime juice, olive oil, sesame oil, mint and sugar in a small bowl and stir until the sugar has dissolved.

Put the prawns in a large bowl, pour over the dressing and toss until the prawns are well coated.

Add the chicken, carrot, snow pea sprouts, cucumber, spring onion and lettuce. Lightly toss together, then pile onto a serving platter or into individual bowls. Sprinkle with the sesame seeds.

prosciutto and papaya salad

SERVES 4

juice of 1 orange
1 teaspoon red wine vinegar
3 tablespoons extra virgin olive oil
2 small red papayas, quartered,
    seeded and peeled
8 slices of prosciutto
15–20 small basil leaves

To make the dressing, put the orange juice, vinegar and olive oil in a small bowl and stir to combine.

Cut the papaya flesh into small wedges and arrange on a serving platter. Tear the prosciutto into bite-sized bits and toss them over the papaya. Scatter the basil leaves over the top.

Stir the dressing again, drizzle it over the salad and serve.

beef carpaccio

300 g (10½ oz) piece of beef
    sirloin, trimmed of fat and sinew
1 egg yolk
1 tablespoon mustard
1 tablespoon lemon juice
150 ml (5 fl oz) light olive oil
2 tablespoons red wine
1 tablespoon salted capers, rinsed,
    drained and finely chopped
2 tablespoons finely chopped
    flat-leaf (Italian) parsley
1 celery stalk, thinly sliced
4 tablespoons dried Asian
    fried shallots (see Note
    on page 109)

Wrap the beef in plastic wrap and put it in the freezer for
30 minutes.

Meanwhile, whisk the egg yolk with the mustard and
lemon juice. Slowly whisk in the olive oil to form a mayonnaise.
Stir through the wine and capers.

Remove the plastic wrap from the chilled beef and, using
a very sharp knife, carefully cut into paper-thin slices.

Arrange the beef slices on four serving plates, garnish
with the parsley, celery and Asian dried shallots. Serve the
mayonnnaise in a bowl on the side; any leftover mayonnaise
can be stored in the refrigerator for 1–2 weeks.

piquant buffalo mozzarella bites

SERVES 4 AS A SIDE DISH

30 g (1 oz/¼ cup) finely chopped
    semi-dried tomatoes
2 tablespoons small salted capers,
    rinsed, drained and finely
    chopped
2 tablespoons finely chopped
    flat-leaf (Italian) parsley
4 large green olives, finely chopped
1 teaspoon finely chopped
    orange zest
2 buffalo mozzarella cheeses
extra virgin olive oil, to serve

Put the semi-dried tomatoes, capers, parsley, olives and orange
zest in a small bowl and toss to combine.

Tear the cheeses into bite-sized pieces and arrange on a
serving plate. Spoon the tomato mixture over the cheese and
season with freshly ground black pepper. Drizzle with the
olive oil and serve.

It's funny how ideas pop out of the cupboard sometimes. Asian fried shallots are normally a condiment added to laksa, salads and rice dishes, however I found myself staring at a jar of them one day and thought how wonderful they would be scattered over beef carpaccio.

Little milky balls of nothingness just crying out for attention. This is a delicious tapas morsel of thickly torn mozzarella with capers, olives, orange zest and semi-dried tomatoes scattered over the top.

Celeriac is one of those vegetables that people are often scared to use. It may well win the title of the ugliest vegetable but its delicate celery flavour works beautifully with rich flavours and creamy dressings.

crab and celeriac remoulade with long toast

....

SERVES 6

2 egg yolks
1 teaspoon dijon mustard
juice of 1 lemon
150 ml (5 fl oz) light olive oil
½ celeriac, peeled and julienned
1 tablespoon finely chopped flat-leaf (Italian) parsley
1 tablespoon snipped chives
150 g (5½ oz) fresh crabmeat
1 long red chilli, seeded and finely chopped
1 sourdough baguette
2 tablespoons extra virgin olive oil
½ teaspoon ground white pepper

Preheat the oven to 150°C (300°F/Gas 2).

Put the egg yolks, mustard and 1 tablespoon of the lemon juice into a large bowl and whisk to combine. Slowly whisk in the light olive oil, a little at a time, until a thick mayonnaise forms.

Add the celeriac, parsley, chives, crabmeat and red chilli. Stir to combine, season to taste with sea salt and freshly ground black pepper, and add more lemon juice if necessary. Transfer to a serving bowl.

Slice the baguette in half lengthways, then thinly slice on an angle to make twelve fingers. Brush the extra virgin olive oil over the long pieces of bread, sprinkle with the white pepper and put them onto an oven tray. Bake for a few minutes on each side until they are crisp and golden brown.

Arrange the toast on a serving platter. Serve with the remoulade, inviting each person to spoon some down the centre of a piece of long toast and season it with a little sea salt and freshly ground black pepper.

salmon ceviche

SERVES 4

500 g (1 lb 2 oz) salmon fillet
juice of 1 orange
juice and finely grated zest of 1 lime
juice of 1 lemon
¼ teaspoon ground white pepper
2 tablespoons finely snipped chives
4 large mint leaves, thinly sliced
extra virgin olive oil, to serve

Finely dice the salmon and put it into a ceramic bowl. Add the orange, lime and lemon juices and the lime zest. Add the white pepper, chives and mint. Stir to combine.

When ready to serve (don't leave the combined salmon and citrus juices too long or the fish may become watery), sprinkle with a little sea salt and spoon into a serving dish. Serve with thin toasts and a drizzle of extra virgin olive oil.

skewered chilli prawns

MAKES 24

2 garlic cloves, crushed
4 bottled jalapeno peppers,
    finely chopped
juice of 1 lime
1 teaspoon dried oregano
1 teaspoon ground cumin
1 teaspoon ground chilli
1 teaspoon honey
2 tablespoons olive oil
24 green prawns, peeled
    and deveined, tails left intact
lime cheeks, to serve

Soak 24 small skewers in water for 30 minutes.

To make the marinade, put the garlic, jalapeno pepper, lime juice, oregano, cumin, chilli and honey into a bowl with the olive oil and stir to combine. Season to taste with sea salt and freshly ground black pepper.

Put one prawn on each skewer and place them in a flat-based container. Pour the marinade over the prawns and marinate for 30 minutes.

Season the prawns with a little sea salt and cook them over a hot barbecue grill or in an oven at 220°C (425°F/Gas 7) for 2–3 minutes on each side (a total of 4–6 minutes).

Serve with a squeeze of lime.

This is a zesty citrus marinade for fish. The white pepper brings a lovely soft heat and the mint and chives add a summer garden freshness to the rich salmon flavours. Serve the ceviche with bread or spooned into lettuce cups.

Nothing says summer more than the smell of prawns sizzling on a barbecue plate. I've put these prawns on skewers but you could forgo the fuss and just pile them onto a plate and serve them as is, or toss them through a simple green salad.

It's funny what kids will eat. My son refuses lasagne but will happily sit down to a feast of these little fish. If you, too, love whitebait, this is a delicious, crunchy bowl full of them.

deep-fried whitebait

SERVES 4–6 AS A STARTER

500 g (1 lb 2 oz) whitebait
125 g (4½ oz/1 cup) plain (all-purpose) flour
1 tablespoon sumac
½ teaspoon cayenne pepper
1 teaspoon sea salt
750 ml (26 fl oz/3 cups) vegetable oil

Rinse the whitebait under cold running water, then drain in a colander or large sieve. Put the flour, sumac, cayenne pepper and sea salt in a large bowl and mix well.

Heat the vegetable oil in a large deep saucepan until the surface begins to shimmer and a pinch of flour dropped into the oil fries immediately.

Pat the whitebait dry with paper towel. Toss them in the seasoned flour, ensuring all the fish are well coated. Lift them out of the bowl and shake off any excess flour, then deep-fry in batches for 3 minutes, or until crisp and golden. Serve with a sprinkle of sea salt.

black bean salsa with tortillas

SERVES 4

2 tablespoons olive oil
1 garlic clove, crushed
1 tablespoon ground cumin
1 red capsicum (pepper), finely diced
200 g (7 oz/1 cup) fresh corn kernels
220 g (7¾ oz/1 cup) cooked black turtle beans (see Note)
25 g (1 oz/½ cup) coarsely chopped coriander (cilantro) leaves
15 g (½ oz/¼ cup) coarsely chopped mint leaves
1 tablespoon pomegranate molasses (see Note)
finely chopped chipotle chilli (see Note) or Tabasco sauce, to taste
rocket (arugula), sour cream and tortillas (optional), to serve

Put the olive oil in a frying pan over medium heat and add the garlic, cumin and capsicum. Sauté until the capsicum is soft, then add the corn and black turtle beans. Cook for a further 5 minutes, or until the corn is golden and soft.

Transfer the corn and bean mixture to a serving bowl. Add the coriander, mint and pomegranate molasses, and season to taste with sea salt, freshly ground black pepper and the chipotle chilli or Tabasco sauce.

Serve as a side dish, or with rocket, sour cream and warm tortillas, if desired.

NOTE: *Black turtle beans are small shiny black beans that are commonly used in Mexican and Cajun cooking. They are available dried from most health stores or cooked and tinned from supermarkets. Pomegranate molasses is a thick syrup made from the reduction of pomegranate juice. It has a bittersweet flavour, which adds a sour bite to many dishes. It is available from Middle Eastern specialty stores. The closest substitute is sweetened tamarind. Chipotle chillies are large jalapeno chillies that have been smoked and dried then cooked in a rich tomato sauce. Tinned chipotle chillies are available from delicatessens and specialty food stores.*

As well as being a tortilla filling, this versatile salad can be served as part of a selection for an outdoor gathering or with warm flat bread, grilled chicken strips and a dollop of sour cream and chilli sauce.

A summery twist on the classic pissaladière. I've discarded the anchovies and added a tumble of tomatoes and basil.

caramelised onion tart

SERVES 4

2 tablespoons butter
2 tablespoons balsamic vinegar
1 teaspoon sugar
8 thyme sprigs
2 red onions, thinly sliced
10 pitted kalamata olives, coarsely chopped
1 sheet frozen puff pastry, thawed
250 g (9 oz) cherry tomatoes, quartered
10 basil leaves

Preheat the oven to 200°C (400°F/Gas 6).

Put the butter, vinegar, sugar and thyme sprigs in a 25 cm (10 inch) ovenproof frying pan over medium heat. Cook for 2–3 minutes, stirring until the sugar has dissolved, then add the onion and stir until coated. Cover with a lid and cook over low heat for 10 minutes, or until the onion is lightly caramelised. Remove the lid and cook for a further 5 minutes to remove most of the liquid.

Remove from the heat, spread the onion evenly in the pan and scatter over the olives. Allow to cool in the frying pan.

Lay the sheet of pastry over the onion and olive mixture in the frying pan, trim to shape, and tuck the edges of the pastry in around the mixture. Bake for 30 minutes, or until the pastry is puffed up and golden brown. Remove from the oven and allow to stand for 5 minutes.

Put a large serving plate over the top of the frying pan and flip the tart and pan upside down. The tart should now be sitting on the plate with the onions and olives facing up. Season to taste with sea salt and freshly ground black pepper.

Top with the tomato quarters and basil and serve with a green salad.

fruit punch

SERVES 8

500 ml (17 fl oz/2 cups) peach nectar
200 ml (7 fl oz) dark rum
3 tablespoons lime juice
3 peaches, peeled and thinly sliced
75 ml (2½ fl oz) ginger syrup (see Note)
160 g (5¾ oz/1 cup) chopped pineapple
1 litre (35 fl oz/4 cups) ginger beer or ginger wine
thinly sliced lime and mint leaves, to garnish

Put all of the ingredients except the garnishes in a large serving or
punch bowl and stir well. Garnish with the lime and mint.

NOTE: *To make the ginger syrup combine ½ cup grated fresh ginger,*
220 g (7¾ oz/1 cup) sugar and 250 ml (9 fl oz/1 cup) water in a small saucepan
and bring to the boil. Reduce the heat and simmer for 2–3 minutes. Strain into
a container, cool and store in the refrigerator until ready to use. This will make
about 250 ml (9 fl oz/1 cup) ginger syrup.

lemonade

SERVES 6–8

2 organic lemons
220 g (7¾ oz/1 cup) sugar
chilled sparkling mineral water, to serve

With a sharp knife, remove strips of peel from the two lemons.
    Juice the lemons. Put the strips of lemon peel in a small saucepan
with the sugar and 125 ml (4 fl oz/½ cup) water. Bring to the boil over
high heat. Reduce the heat and simmer for a few minutes, then remove
from the heat and allow to cool. Discard the lemon peel strips and add
the lemon juice.
    Serve diluted to taste with the sparkling mineral water.

Since I was a child we've always made versions of this punch for large family gatherings. It is loved by children and adults alike and is packed with summery flavours. For the children's version, forgo the rum and use extra ginger beer.

Who can argue with home-made lemonade on a summer's afternoon? So much more tangy than the commercial variety, this is the perfect drink when you want to surprise and refresh your guests.

This peachy perfect cake is best made in late summer when the peaches are full flavoured and juicy. It can be served for afternoon tea or with a generous dollop of cream for dessert.

peach cake

4 eggs, separated
155 g (5½ oz/1¼ cups) plain (all-purpose) flour
1 teaspoon baking powder
150 g (5½ oz/⅔ cup) caster (superfine) sugar
120 g (4¼ oz) unsalted butter, melted
1 tablespoon grated lemon zest
500 g (1 lb 2 oz/about 3) ripe peaches, peeled
    and cut into thick wedges
icing (confectioners') sugar, for dusting

Preheat the oven to 180°C (350°F/Gas 4). Grease and line a 23 cm (9 inch) spring-form cake tin.

In a bowl, whisk the egg whites using electric beaters until soft peaks form. Sift the flour and baking powder into another bowl, then add the sugar. Stir to combine, then make a well in the centre. In another bowl, whisk together the butter, egg yolks and lemon zest. Stir the liquid ingredients and one-third of the egg whites into the dry ingredients to form a smooth batter, then fold the remaining egg whites through.

Pour the batter into the prepared cake tin. Arrange the peach slices in a single layer over the top and bake for 30–40 minutes, or until the cake is golden brown and a skewer inserted into the centre comes out clean. Allow to cool, then turn the cake out of the tin and dust with icing sugar.

white velvet cake with passionfruit

SERVES 8

135 g (4¾ oz) white chocolate
125 g (4½ oz) unsalted butter
4 eggs, separated
90 g (3¼ oz) sugar
60 g (2¼ oz/½ cup) plain (all-purpose) flour
200 ml (7 fl oz) thin (pouring/whipping)
    cream, whipped
pulp of 4 passionfruit

Preheat the oven to 180°C (350°F/Gas 4). Grease a 20 cm (8 inch) round cake tin and line it with baking paper.

Put the chocolate and butter into a bowl over a small saucepan of water and melt over very low heat. (Make sure the base of the bowl does not touch the water.) Remove from the heat. With electric beaters, whisk the egg whites until soft peaks form, then add the sugar and continue to whisk until the whites are firm and glossy.

Transfer the warm chocolate mixture to a large bowl and add the egg yolks, one at a time, while constantly whisking. Add the flour to the chocolate mixture and gently stir to combine. Gently fold together the chocolate mixture and the egg whites. Spoon the batter into the prepared cake tin and bake for 20 minutes, or until firm.

Allow the cake to cool in the tin, then turn it out onto a serving plate. Spoon whipped cream over the top of the cake and drizzle with the passionfruit pulp.

The white chocolate in this recipe gives this cake a rich flavour and texture that is offset by the tangy passionfruit. You could also top it with fresh raspberries or strawberries.

There are only a few months of the year when fresh apricots taste like they should. When the time is right, grab as many as you can and use them for jam, summer crumbles and tarts like this one. For this recipe the apricots should be soft-fleshed and sweet.

apricot tart

SERVES 6

100 g (3½ oz/1 heaped cup) flaked almonds
1 tablespoon butter
1 egg
3 tablespoons honey
8 small ripe apricots, halved and stones removed
icing (confectioners') sugar, to serve
vanilla ice cream, to serve

fruit tart base
2½ tablespoons unsalted butter
3 tablespoons sour cream
125 g (4½ oz/1 cup) plain (all-purpose) flour
1 heaped teaspoon caster (superfine) sugar

Preheat the oven to 160°C (315°F/Gas 2–3). Line a baking tray with baking paper. Put all of the ingredients for the fruit tart base in a food processor and chop until the pastry begins to come together. Remove from the processor, form into a flat disc, cover in plastic wrap and refrigerate for 10 minutes.

Wipe the processor bowl clean and add the flaked almonds, butter, egg and honey. Process to a thick, uneven paste.

Roll out the chilled pastry between two sheets of baking paper to form a 30 cm (12 inch) square. Lay the pastry on the baking tray and create an edge for the finished tart by rolling over 1 cm (½ inch) of pastry all the way round.

Spread the almond mixture over the pastry, then arrange the apricot halves over the top, cut side up. Cover with foil and bake for 30 minutes, then remove the foil and bake for a further 15 minutes. Dust with icing sugar and serve as slices with vanilla ice cream.

mango jellies with summer fruit salad

SERVES 4

1 large ripe mango, diced
juice of 2 limes
115 g (4 oz/½ cup) caster
(superfine) sugar
375 ml (13 fl oz/1½ cups)
fresh orange juice, plus juice
of 1 orange, extra
3 teaspoons powdered gelatine
200 g (7 oz/1 cup) finely
diced pineapple
1 ripe peach, halved, stone removed
and cut into wedges
pulp of 2 passionfruit
sansho pepper, optional (see Note)

To make the mango jellies, purée the mango in a blender with the lime juice. Pour the mixture into a measuring container — you will need 250 ml (9 fl oz/1 cup) of liquid; if you don't have quite enough, top up with water or orange juice. Set aside.

Put the sugar and fresh orange juice into a small saucepan over medium heat. Stir until the sugar has dissolved, then pour the liquid into a bowl. Sprinkle the gelatine over the warm liquid and stir for 1–2 minutes, or until evenly dissolved. Stir in the mango purée, then ladle into four 150 ml (5 fl oz) jelly moulds or ramekins. Cover with plastic wrap and refrigerate overnight.

Just before serving, put the pineapple, peach, passionfruit pulp and extra orange juice in a bowl and gently mix together. Dip the moulds in hot water, then turn the jellies out onto four serving plates. Spoon the fruit salad around them and sprinkle with a little sansho pepper, if desired.

NOTE: *Sansho pepper is also known as 'Japanese pepper' and is commonly used as a seasoning in Japanese cooking.*

If you can find sansho pepper, it will add a quirky extra flavour to what is already a bowl of summery goodness.

With its subtle coconut flavour and creamy texture, this bavarois makes me dream of swaying palms and shimmering blue horizons.

coconut and passionfruit bavarois

SERVES 4

250 ml (9 fl oz/1 cup) thin (pouring/whipping) cream
300 ml (10½ fl oz) milk
45 g (1½ oz/½ cup) desiccated coconut
125 g (4½ oz/heaped ½ cup) caster (superfine) sugar
4 egg yolks
1 teaspoon powdered gelatine
4 passionfruit
almond bread or biscotti, to serve (optional)

Whip the cream in a bowl, cover with plastic wrap and refrigerate until needed.

Put the milk into a heavy-based saucepan over very low heat and stir in the coconut and sugar. Allow to just simmer for 15 minutes, or until reduced and thick. Strain the liquid into a bowl, using the back of a large spoon to press as much liquid as possible out of the coconut.

Whisk the egg yolks in a separate bowl. Whisk in the warm milk mixture. Pour into a clean saucepan and stir over medium heat for 8–10 minutes, or until the mixture coats the back of the spoon. Pour into a clean bowl.

In a small bowl, dissolve the gelatine powder in 2 tablespoons boiling water. Stir well, until the gelatine crystals have completely dissolved. Pour the dissolved gelatine into the warm milk and stir until thoroughly blended. Leave for about 45 minutes, or until cool.

Fold the whipped cream through the mixture and spoon into four serving glasses. Cover with plastic wrap and refrigerate for 3 hours, or overnight.

Just before serving, cut the passionfruit in half, scoop out the seeds and spoon them over the top. Serve with almond bread or biscotti, if desired.

strawberry and tarragon jelly

SERVES 4–6

500 g (1 lb 2 oz/3⅓ cups) strawberries, hulled and sliced, plus extra chopped strawberries, to serve
175 g (6 oz/¾ cup) caster (superfine) sugar
1 tablespoon finely chopped tarragon
2 heaped tablespoons powdered gelatine
crème anglais or thin (pouring/whipping) cream, to serve

Combine the strawberries, sugar and tarragon in a bowl, stirring well. Cover and leave to macerate for 30 minutes.

Blend the strawberry mixture in a food processor or blender with 125 ml (4 fl oz/½ cup) water, then strain into a large measuring container.

Sprinkle the gelatine over 250 ml (9 fl oz/1 cup) hot water and stir for 1–2 minutes, or until thoroughly dissolved, then stir into the strawberry juice. Add just enough warm water to make 1 litre (35 fl oz/4 cups) of liquid. Leave to cool.

Pour the liquid into a large bowl and cover with plastic wrap. Refrigerate for several hours or overnight to set the jelly.

To serve, spoon the jelly into tall glasses and drizzle with crème anglais or cream. Scatter over the chopped strawberries.

This jelly sets a little cloudy but don't worry, all the delicious strawberry bits give it a yummy flavour. Speaking of flavour, trust me with the tarragon – it's a surprising herby hit that works really well.

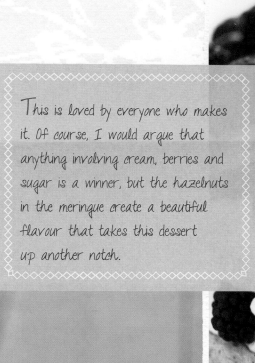

This is loved by everyone who makes it. Of course, I would argue that anything involving cream, berries and sugar is a winner, but the hazelnuts in the meringue create a beautiful flavour that takes this dessert up another notch.

I love home-made ice desserts but since I don't have an ice cream machine I almost always write recipes like this one that don't involve churning. This semifreddo is richly sweet with the flavours of fig and honey.

hazelnut meringue with berries

SERVES 6

2 egg whites
115 g (4 oz/½ cup) caster (superfine) sugar
4 tablespoons ground hazelnuts
310 ml (10¾ fl oz/1¼ cups) thin (pouring/whipping) cream
1 teaspoon natural vanilla extract
3 punnets (about 450 g/1 lb) mixed strawberries, raspberries
    and blackberries, strawberries quartered

Preheat the oven to 150°C (300°F/Gas 2). Whisk the egg whites until they form soft peaks. Slowly add the sugar, continuing to whisk until the mixture is stiff. Fold in the ground hazelnuts.

Line two baking trays with baking paper and divide the meringue between them, putting a big dollop in the middle of each tray. Using the back of a spoon, spread the mixture out until you have two 20 cm (8 inch) circles of meringue.

Bake for 40 minutes. Turn the oven off, but leave the meringues in the oven, with the door ajar, for 30 minutes.

Whip the cream and fold in the vanilla. When the meringues are cool, put one of the rounds on a serving plate and top with some of the cream and half the berries, arranging them so that they make an even surface for the next meringue layer. Put the other meringue on top and decorate with remaining the cream and berries. Allow to sit for 15 minutes before serving.

peach and fig semifreddo

SERVES 6

4 egg yolks
150 g (5½ oz) honey
300 ml (10½ fl oz) thin (pouring/whipping) cream
2 peaches, diced, plus extra wedges, to serve (optional)
5 dried figs, finely chopped
fresh fruit, to serve

Line a 10 x 20 cm (4 x 8 inch) loaf (bar) tin with plastic wrap.

Whisk the egg yolks with the honey until light and frothy. Whip the cream until it forms soft peaks, then fold it into the honey mixture. Stir in the peach and fig. Pour into the prepared tin, cover with plastic wrap and freeze overnight.

When ready to serve, turn the semifreddo out onto a serving plate and cut into thick slices. Serve with fresh fruit.

SUMMER

sunshine and stars

There really is something special about those summer days when the long afternoons blend seamlessly into the starry evenings. It's funny how whenever anyone mentions summer I always think of holidays by the seaside and never the muggy rush through the city on my way to work. It's always memories of endless golden days when the sun finally sets over a dinner table laden with food, where gossipy tales are exchanged with friends over chilled drinks, the children run barefoot in the backyard and everyone is a little salty and sun-kissed. To reflect this, summer food need only be simple with touches of the exotic, light and fresh, and easily shared.

soupy mussels

SERVES 4

1 kg (2 lb 4 oz) mussels
1 tablespoon olive oil
1 leek, white part only, rinsed and finely chopped
2 garlic cloves, finely chopped
¼ teaspoon cayenne pepper
½ teaspoon ground cumin
1 tablespoon finely grated fresh ginger
400 g (14 oz) tin chopped tomatoes
200 ml (7 fl oz) coconut cream
a handful coriander (cilantro) leaves

Clean the mussels in the sink under cold running water, scrubbing them to remove any barnacles or bits of hairy 'beard'. Throw away any that are open and that do not close when you tap them on the work surface.

Heat the olive oil in a large frying pan over medium heat and cook the leek and garlic until soft and golden brown. Add the cayenne pepper, cumin and ginger. Cook for a further minute, add the tomatoes and bring to the boil. Add the mussels, cover and steam for 8–10 minutes, or until all of the mussels have opened. Discard any unopened mussels.

Divide the mussels among four warm bowls.

Add 200 ml (7 fl oz) water to the pan and return to the boil. Once the soupy mixture has boiled, remove the pan from the heat and stir in the coconut cream. To serve, ladle the mixture over the mussels and scatter over the coriander leaves.

I ate some amazing spicy mussels by a beach once and I was so swayed by the moonlight on the water and the salty breeze that I always think of such locations when eating them.

The finely chopped avocado salsa on these lightly cooked scallops brings a limey coriander bite to the delicate scallops. The salsa is also a perfect accompaniment to barbecued fish.

This is a beautiful chilled tomato soup flavoured with cumin, white pepper and fresh ginger. If you have problems getting your head around the idea of a cold soup, think of it as a Virgin Mary in a bowl!

baked scallops with avocado salsa

....

SERVES 4

1 avocado, finely diced
2 tablespoons finely chopped coriander (cilantro) leaves
1 large red chilli, seeded and finely chopped
1 tablespoon lime juice
1 teaspoon light olive oil
16 scallops, cleaned and on the half shell
1 tablespoon softened butter

Preheat the oven to 200°C (400°F/Gas 6).

In a bowl, combine the avocado, coriander, chilli, lime juice and olive oil. Season lightly with sea salt and freshly ground black pepper. Set aside.

Place the scallops on a baking tray and dab each one with a little butter. Bake in the oven for 2–3 minutes.

Arrange the scallops on a serving platter. Spoon over the salsa and serve.

chilled tomato soup

....

SERVES 4

2 teaspoons sea salt
1 teaspoon ground cumin
½ teaspoon ground white pepper
1 tablespoon finely grated fresh ginger
2 tablespoons olive oil
10 large vine-ripened tomatoes
10 small mint leaves, plus extra, to serve
125 ml (4 fl oz/½ cup) dry sherry

Preheat the oven to 180°C (350°F/Gas 4). In a small bowl, combine the sea salt, cumin, white pepper, ginger and olive oil.

Using a small, sharp knife, remove the stem of one tomato with a circular action to make a crater in the top. Repeat with the other tomatoes and sit them on a baking tray. Fill the top of each tomato with the salt mixture, then bake for 30 minutes, or until they are soft and starting to split. Allow to cool.

Coarsely chop the tomatoes and put them in a blender or food processor along with the mint. Blend to a purée, strain into a large bowl and stir in the sherry. Cover with plastic wrap and chill until ready to serve.

Spoon into four bowls and scatter over the mint leaves.

saffron rice with garlic prawns

SERVES 4

¼ teaspoon saffron threads
200 g (7 oz/1 cup) basmati rice
250 g (9 oz) cherry tomatoes, halved
2 tablespoons olive oil
2 onions, diced
3 whole cloves
300 ml (10½ fl oz) chicken stock
40 g (1½ oz) butter
3 garlic cloves, crushed
20 raw king prawns (shrimp), peeled and deveined, tails left intact
a handful coriander (cilantro) leaves

Put the saffron threads in a small bowl with 1 tablespoon hot water. Set aside.

Rinse the rice several times, then put in a bowl and cover with water.

Squeeze out the seeds from the tomatoes and discard them.

Put a large heavy-based saucepan over medium heat and add the olive oil, onion and cloves. Cook until the onion is soft. Drain the rice and add it to the saucepan along with the chicken stock and the saffron mixture. Season with some sea salt. Bring to the boil, stirring to ensure that the rice does not settle. Reduce the heat to medium and simmer, partially covered, for 10 minutes or until most of the liquid has been absorbed. Remove from the heat and cover tightly. Allow to sit for 10 minutes.

Heat the butter in a heavy-based frying pan and add the garlic. When the butter is sizzling, add the prawns, a few at a time, and cook for a few minutes on each side, removing to a warm plate as they are done. When all of the prawns have been cooked, add the tomatoes to the garlicky butter, season with a little sea salt and cook until soft.

Spoon the rice into four bowls and top with the coriander, prawns and tomatoes. Drizzle with the garlicky juices and serve.

I always think wet rice dishes are instantly comforting. Since this is served with prawns and squishy roast tomatoes, I'm going to call it summer comfort in a bowl.

This is simply a noodle version of a Thai beef salad. Flavoured with chilli, lemongrass and ginger, this cool noodle salad is the perfect pick-me-up at the end of a long day.

seared beef and noodle salad

....

SERVES 4

zest and juice of 2 limes
zest and juice of 1 orange
2 tablespoons fish sauce
1 teaspoon sesame oil
1 tablespoon grated palm sugar (jaggery) or light brown sugar
1 garlic clove, crushed
2 tablespoons finely chopped lemongrass, white part only
1 tablespoon julienned fresh ginger
1 large red chilli, seeded and thinly sliced
2 tablespoons olive oil
250 g (9 oz) piece of beef sirloin
200 g (7 oz) somen noodles
a handful coriander (cilantro) leaves
a handful Thai basil

To make the dressing, in a small bowl mix together the lime zest and juice, orange zest and juice, fish sauce, sesame oil, sugar, garlic, lemongrass, ginger and chilli. Stir until the sugar has dissolved, then cover and set aside.

Heat the olive oil in a frying pan over high heat and cook the beef for 2–3 minutes, or until well seared, on each side. Transfer the meat to a bowl, cover loosely with foil and leave to rest.

Bring a large saucepan of salted water to the boil. Add the noodles and cook for 2 minutes, then drain and rinse under running water. Put the noodles in a large bowl and pour half of the dressing over. Toss well to coat.

Divide the noodles among four bowls. Thinly slice the beef and arrange over the noodles. Scatter with the coriander and basil and spoon the remaining dressing over the top.

somen noodle salad with seared prawns

SERVES 4

300 g (10½ oz) somen noodles
2 handfuls mint leaves
2 handfuls coriander (cilantro) leaves
12 cm (4½ inch) piece of daikon radish,
    (see Note on page 53),
    peeled and julienned
1 tablespoon olive oil
1 tablespoon lime juice
16 raw king prawns (shrimp), peeled and
    deveined, tails left intact

soy and sesame dressing
3 tablespoons soy sauce
3 tablespoons sesame oil
1½ tablespoons balsamic vinegar
2 tablespoons sugar
2 tablespoons lime juice
1 teaspoon finely grated fresh ginger
1 tablespoon finely chopped lemongrass,
    white part only

To make the dressing, put all of the ingredients in a large bowl and stir until the sugar has dissolved. Set aside.

Bring a large saucepan of water to the boil and cook the noodles until *al dente*. Drain and rinse under cold running water, then toss the noodles in the dressing until well coated. Add the mint, coriander and daikon to the noodles, and toss again. Pile the noodle mixture into four serving bowls.

Combine the olive oil and lime juice in a bowl. Add the prawns and toss until well coated.

Heat a large non-stick frying pan over high heat. When the pan is hot, sear the prawns on both sides for 1–2 minutes, until they turn pink and begin to curl up. Arrange over the noodles and serve immediately.

Slippery slidey Asian-style noodles are not a first-date ingredient, but they are fun to eat. These are flavoured with a soy and sesame dressing that has been a favourite of mine for years. I used to make a big jar of it to have in the refrigerator for any quick pick-me-up noodle meal.

Because I love fresh flavours, I'm a big fan of the uncooked pasta sauce – perfect ingredients melded with oil and herbs. In this instance, the crab could be replaced with tinned tuna, prosciutto, grilled prawns or just big chunks of fresh tomato, and still taste fabulous.

This couscous salad looks so beautifully alive with the colours of summer, you can almost see the striped umbrellas and hear the ocean.

crab and chilli pasta

SERVES 4

350 g (12 oz) fresh crabmeat
2 large red chillies, seeded and finely chopped
grated zest and juice of 1 lemon
80 ml (2½ fl oz/⅓ cup) extra virgin olive oil
a handful flat-leaf (Italian) parsley, coarsely chopped
150 g (5½ oz/3⅓ cups) baby rocket (arugula) leaves
300 g (10½ oz) linguine

Put the crabmeat in a large bowl and coarsely flake it with a fork. Add the chilli, lemon zest and juice, and olive oil. Season liberally with sea salt and freshly ground black pepper. Stir to combine. Pile the parsley and rocket on top.

Bring a large saucepan of salted water to the boil and add the linguine. Cook until *al dente*, then drain and add to the crab mixture. Toss well until the rocket has wilted. Divide among four warmed pasta bowls.

couscous with herbs and chickpeas

SERVES 4

185 g (6½ oz/1 cup) instant couscous
1 teaspoon butter
400 g (14 oz) tin chickpeas, drained and rinsed
2 ripe roma (plum) tomatoes, seeded and diced
½ red onion, finely diced
10 g (¼ oz/½ cup) mint leaves
15 g (½ oz/½ cup) coriander (cilantro) leaves
10 g (¼ oz/½ cup) flat-leaf (Italian) parsley leaves
2 tablespoons diced preserved lemon rind
1 tablespoon lemon juice
3 tablespoons olive oil

Put the couscous in a large bowl with the butter and cover with 250 ml (9 fl oz/1 cup) boiling water. Cover and leave the couscous for 10 minutes, separating the grains with a fork after 5 minutes.

Rub the couscous grains between your fingers to break up any lumps, then add the remaining ingredients. Toss, season with sea salt and freshly ground black pepper and serve.

salmon wrapped in vine leaves

SERVES 4

> 4 x 150 g (5½ oz) salmon fillets, pin-boned
>   and skin removed
> 16 preserved vine leaves
> 250 g (9 oz) cherry tomatoes
> 185 g (6½ oz/1 cup) instant couscous
> 1 tablespoon butter
> a handful flat-leaf (Italian) parsley,
>   coarsely chopped
> 2 spring onions (scallions), thinly sliced
> extra virgin olive oil, to serve
> lemon wedges, to serve

Preheat the oven to 200°C (400°F/Gas 6). Rinse the salmon fillets and pat dry with paper towel. Rinse the vine leaves several times to remove some of the saltiness, but leave them slightly wet to make them easier to work with.

Lay four vine leaves on a clean surface with their edges generously overlapping. Lay a salmon fillet in the middle, then wrap the leaves around the fish. Repeat with the remaining vine leaves and salmon fillets to make four parcels. Put them on a baking tray with the whole cherry tomatoes and bake for 15 minutes.

Meanwhile, put the couscous and butter in a large bowl and pour 250 ml (9 fl oz/1 cup) boiling water over the top. Cover and allow to sit for 5 minutes, then fluff up the grains with a fork. Cover again and leave for a further 5 minutes. When the couscous has absorbed all the water, rub the grains with your fingertips to remove any lumps.

Add the roasted cherry tomatoes to the couscous along with the parsley and spring onion. Lightly toss together.

Divide the salmon parcels among four warmed plates and peel the vine leaves open. Spoon the couscous over the middle of the salmon and serve with a drizzle of olive oil and lemon wedges.

I love cooking with vine leaves and I think this is partly an aesthetic response to the beautiful dark green leaves, and possibly also happy distant memories of Greek holidays. In the here and now, the briny flavour of the leaves complements the rich salmon, and encasing the fish in the leaves allows it to cook beautifully.

Ginger and white pepper give depth and heat to the sweet sauce, while the fresh mint leaves and lime juice bring the whole dish alive. Serve with steamed rice, noodles or an Asian-style salad.

caramelised chicken breasts

3 tablespoons vegetable oil
4 boneless chicken breast fillets, skin on
3 French or red Asian shallots, finely chopped
3 tablespoons caster (superfine) sugar
3 tablespoons fish sauce
1 tablespoon finely grated fresh ginger
¼ teaspoon ground white pepper
2 small Lebanese (short) cucumbers, thinly sliced
2 witlof (chicory/Belgian endive), leaves separated
25 g (1 oz/1 bunch) chives, finely snipped
20 mint leaves
1 tablespoon lime juice
steamed white rice, to serve

Heat the oil in a large heavy-based frying pan over medium–high heat. Add the chicken, skin side down, and cook for 3 minutes, or until golden brown. Turn and cook the other sides for 2 minutes, then remove the chicken from the pan.

Add the shallots to the pan and cook for 1 minute over medium heat. Add the sugar and cook for a further 2 minutes, or until the shallots are golden brown. Stir in the fish sauce, ginger and white pepper and cook for 1 minute.

Return the chicken to the pan, skin side up. Cover, reduce the heat to low and cook for 12–15 minutes, or until the chicken is cooked through. Take the pan off the heat and keep the chicken warm while preparing the salad.

In a bowl, toss together the cucumber, witlof, chives, mint and lime juice. Season with sea salt.

Thickly slice the chicken breasts across the grain. Arrange the salad and chicken on top of the steamed rice in four bowls. Spoon the caramelised shallots and pan juices over the chicken just before serving.

coconut and green bean salad

SERVES 4 AS A SIDE DISH

400 g (14 oz) green beans
2 green chillies, finely chopped
1 teaspoon finely grated
    fresh ginger
95 g (3¼ oz/⅓ cup) plain yoghurt
juice of 1 lime
1 teaspoon sea salt
¼ coconut, flesh freshly shaved
2 tablespoons vegetable oil
1 tablespoon brown mustard seeds
30 curry leaves

Bring a saucepan of water to the boil and cook the beans for 2–3 minutes, or until they are brilliant green. Drain and refresh under cold running water. Drain again.

Put the chilli, ginger, yoghurt, lime juice and sea salt in a bowl, add the coconut and toss to combine.

Heat the oil in a small frying pan over medium heat. Add the mustard seeds and curry leaves, and when the seeds begin to pop remove the pan from the heat.

Add the seeds and leaves to the coconut mixture and toss to combine. Stir through the green beans.

aromatic roast chicken breasts

SERVES 4

1 vanilla bean
2 tablespoons soy sauce
2 tablespoons grated palm sugar
    (jaggery) or light brown sugar
2 tablespoons grated lemon zest
4 chicken breast fillets, skin on
juice of 4 lemons
80 ml (2½ fl oz/⅓ cup) olive oil
185 g (6½ oz/1 cup) instant
    couscous
1 tablespoon butter
1 tablespoon corsely chopped
    flat-leaf (Italian) parsley
1 tablespoon finely chopped mint
50 g (1¾ oz) snow pea
    (mangetout) shoots

Preheat the oven to 200°C (400°F/Gas 6). Using a sharp knife, slice the vanilla bean in half lengthways and scrape the seeds into a bowl (reserve the vanilla pod for another use). Add the soy sauce, sugar and lemon zest and stir to combine.

Using a sharp knife, cut several long incisions into the skin of each chicken breast, then rub the soy mixture into the skin. Put the lemon juice and olive oil in a small casserole dish or baking dish and add the chicken breasts, skin side up. Roast for 15 minutes, or until the chicken is cooked through.

Meanwhile, put the couscous and butter in a bowl and pour over 250ml (9 fl oz/1 cup) boiling water. Cover and set aside for 5 minutes, then fluff up the grains with a fork. Cover again and leave for a further 5 minutes. Season with a little sea salt and freshly ground black pepper, then fold through the parsley and mint.

Carve the chicken into thick slices. Arrange over the snow pea shoots and serve with the couscous, with the baking juices spooned over the top.

Many years ago in London, I was taken to my first restaurant that specialised in the cuisine of Southern India. After far too many heavy Anglicised curries it was a revelation to eat this intense, fresh and lively food. This is a fresh bean and coconut salad in the spirit of the south.

I wrote this recipe while I was reading a book about the history of vanilla. I was so entranced by the whole vanilla saga and so inspired reading about savoury vanilla recipes that I had to have a play with this wonderful ingredient.

Coconut cream is used in Asian cooking to bring a rich creaminess to the often spicy and hot flavour bases. Which made me think it would be simply lovely mixed through a flavour-packed salsa.

Not exactly a one-pot dinner, but close. I always love a meal that has this much impact and so little effort. Even if you don't normally like anchovies, don't remove them from the recipe as they add a nice rich saltiness to the tomatoes and beans.

red snapper with tomato salsa

SERVES 4

2 tablespoons vegetable oil

4 x 200 g (7 oz) red snapper
  fillets, skin on

lime wedges, to serve

tomato salsa

250 g (9 oz) cherry tomatoes,
  quartered

1 teaspoon finely grated
  fresh ginger

2 tablespoons finely diced
  red onion

6 basil leaves, thinly sliced

1½ tablespoons lime juice

1½ tablespoons coconut cream

Preheat the oven to 200°C (400°F/Gas 6). Put all of the tomato salsa ingredients into a small bowl. Mix together and set aside.

Put the vegetable oil in a large heavy-based frying pan over high heat. Rinse the snapper fillets and pat dry with paper towels. Season generously with sea salt and sit the fillets, skin side down, in the hot pan. Sear for 1–2 minutes, or until the skin is crisp and golden, then turn the fillets over.

Transfer the fish, skin side up, onto a baking tray lined with foil. Bake for 8–10 minutes, or until cooked through. Lift the fillets onto serving plates, then spoon the tomato salsa over the top and serve with lime wedges.

rack of lamb with spinach and white beans

SERVES 4

6 ripe roma (plum) tomatoes,
  halved

500 g (1 lb 2 oz/1 bunch) English
  spinach, rinsed and trimmed

400 g (14 oz) tin cannellini (white)
  beans, drained and rinsed

250 ml (9 fl oz/1 cup) veal or
  beef stock

4 anchovy fillets

2 x 8 piece racks of lamb, trimmed

Preheat the oven to 190°C (375°F/Gas 5). Put the tomatoes in a deep roasting tin. Roast for 30 minutes, or until the tomatoes are beginning to darken and shrivel. Meanwhile, blanch the spinach in boiling water for 2–3 minutes, then drain and coarsely chop.

Add the spinach, beans and stock to the roasting tin. Break the anchovies into small pieces and scatter over the vegetables.

Heat a large frying pan over high heat and sear the lamb racks on all sides for 2–3 minutes, or until browned. Put the racks into the roasting tin and return to the oven for 20 minutes. Remove the roasting tin from the oven and cover with foil. Allow to rest for 10 minutes.

Arrange the vegetables on four warmed plates. Slice the racks into individual cutlets and arrange them over the vegetables. Spoon over the roasting juices and serve.

lemon and parmesan spaghettini

SERVES 4

juice and finely grated zest
   of 2 lemons
400 g (14 oz) spaghettini
3 tablespoons olive oil
2 garlic cloves, finely chopped
2 leeks, white part only, rinsed and
   thinly sliced
2 tablespoons small salted capers,
   rinsed and drained
a handful flat-leaf (Italian) parsley,
   coarsely chopped
25 g (1 oz/1 bunch) chives,
   finely snipped
70 g (2½ oz/½ cup) finely grated
   parmesan cheese

Bring a large saucepan of salted water to the boil and add half of the lemon juice. Cook the spaghettini until *al dente*, then drain and return it to the warm pan.

Meanwhile, heat the olive oil in a large frying pan over medium heat. Add the garlic and leek and sauté until the leek is soft and translucent. Season with a little freshly ground black pepper.

Add the mixture to the pan with the pasta, along with the lemon zest and remaining lemon juice, capers, parsley and chives. Stir the mixture well and divide among four warmed pasta bowls. Sprinkle with the parmesan cheese and serve immediately.

burger with beetroot slices

SERVES 4

4 beetroot (beets)
1 tablespoon balsamic vinegar
1 tablespoon brown sugar
6 mint leaves, thinly sliced
1 large red chilli, seeded and
   finely chopped
500 g (1 lb 2 oz) minced (ground)
   pork and veal
1 teaspoon finely grated
   fresh ginger
1 tablespoon finely chopped
   lemongrass, white part only
½ onion, finely diced
1 tablespoon soy sauce
2 tablespoons tomato paste
   (concentrated purée)
½ trimmed iceberg lettuce,
   thinly sliced
4 soft burger rolls, split open
a handful coriander (cilantro) leaves

Put the beetroot in a saucepan and cover with cold water. Bring to the boil and cook for 30 minutes, or until the beetroot is cooked through. Drain and allow to cool. Wearing rubber gloves, rub the skins from the beetroot, then thinly slice the beetroot into a bowl.

In a small bowl, mix together the vinegar, brown sugar, mint and chilli, stirring until the sugar has dissolved. Pour the dressing over the beetroot and set aside.

Put the minced meat, ginger, lemongrass, onion, soy sauce and tomato paste in a large bowl. Season with sea salt and freshly ground black pepper. Knead the ingredients together with your hands then form it into four large patties.

Heat a barbecue grill or large non-stick frying pan over high heat and sear the patties. With a spatula, press down to flatten them, before reducing the heat to medium and cooking for 5 minutes. Flip the patties over and continue to cook until the meat is cooked through.

Put the lettuce onto the open burger rolls and top with the burger, beetroot slices and coriander leaves.

To make life easy there are a few must-have ingredients that should be in every kitchen. In the pantry a selection of dried pastas, anchovies and capers, tinned chickpeas, white beans and tomatoes and extra virgin olive oil. To this, I'd add parmesan, eggs, lemons and herbs in the refrigerator.

The great Aussie hamburger is never complete without a few slices of vinegary beetroot, and this is a home-made twist on the theme. Freshly cooked beetroot is sliced and dressed with mint and chilli and the burger meat is flavoured with lemongrass, ginger and soy.

The trick to this salad is to shred the chicken meat finely so that all the flavours come together in one mouthful. The anchovy mayonnaise would also work well on a simple green salad to serve with barbecued lamb or veal.

chicken and pine nut salad

SERVES 4

1 tablespoon sea salt
2 skinless chicken breast fillets
1 egg yolk
zest and juice of 1 lemon
125 ml (4 fl oz/½ cup) light olive oil
2 anchovy fillets, finely chopped
3 tablespoons small salted capers,
    rinsed and drained
3 tablespoons toasted pine nuts
3 tablespoons currants
1 very large handful flat-leaf (Italian)
    parsley, coarsely chopped
warm crusty bread, to serve

Put a large saucepan of water over high heat, add the sea salt and bring to the boil. Add the chicken breasts, then cover the saucepan and remove it from the heat. Set aside for 40 minutes to allow the residual heat to gently poach the chicken. Lift the chicken out of the water and allow to cool, then shred the meat.

In a small bowl, whisk together the egg yolk and lemon juice. Slowly add the olive oil, whisking constantly to form a thick, creamy mayonnaise. Fold the anchovies through and season with sea salt and freshly ground black pepper.

Put the chicken, lemon zest, capers, pine nuts, currants and parsley in a large bowl and toss to combine. Stir the anchovy mayonnaise through the salad, then spoon into four bowls and serve with warm crusty bread.

poached chicken salad

90 g (3¼ oz/1 bunch) coriander (cilantro)
4 spring onions (scallions)
1 tablespoon sea salt
2 skinless chicken breast fillets
2–3 red capsicums (peppers)
80 ml (2½ fl oz/⅓ cup) olive oil
1 tablespoon balsamic vinegar
½ teaspoon smoked paprika
1 telegraph (long) cucumber, peeled and diced
couscous, prepared following packet directions, to serve

Put a large saucepan of water over high heat. Add two of the coriander sprigs, two whole spring onions and the sea salt and bring to the boil. Add the chicken breasts, then cover the saucepan and remove it from the heat. Set aside for 40 minutes to allow the residual heat to gently poach the chicken.

Meanwhile, cut the capsicum into large flattish pieces and remove the seeds and membrane. Cook, skin side up, under a hot grill (broiler) until the skin blackens and blisters. Cool in a plastic bag, then peel off the skin. Cut the flesh into strips.

Put the capsicum into a bowl with the olive oil, vinegar and paprika. Season with sea salt and freshly ground black pepper and toss until well combined. Pick the coriander leaves from the remaining sprigs and add a good handful to the capsicum. Coarsely chop the remaining spring onions and add them to the salad, along with the cucumber.

Lift the chicken out of the poaching water and thinly slice against the grain. Add to the salad and toss to combine. Serve with couscous.

When roasted, red capsicums become rich and sweet and a little bit smoky. It's these flavours that bring a little depth to this salad of poached chicken and fresh herbs, making it a lovely light but flavoursome summery dish.

If you are lucky enough to have a Chinatown nearby or a shop selling Chinese roast ducks, then this salad is for you. Crispy skin, juicy meat, sweet mango, crunchy water chestnuts and the peppery bite of watercress.

duck salad

SERVES 4–6

2 tablespoons tamarind purée (see Note on page 79)
1 teaspoon soy sauce
2 teaspoons finely grated fresh ginger
1 tablespoon grated palm sugar (jaggery) or light brown sugar
½ teaspoon ground cumin
1 large red chilli, seeded and finely chopped
1 Chinese roasted duck
2 ripe mangoes, cut into thin strips
500 g (1 lb 2 oz/1 large bunch) watercress, leaves picked
200 g (7 oz) tin water chestnuts, drained and sliced

Put the tamarind purée in a large bowl, add 3 tablespoons water and stir. To make the dressing, combine the tamarind water, soy sauce, ginger, sugar, cumin and chilli in a large bowl. Stir and set aside.

Pull the skin off the duck and cut it into thin strips, scraping off any fat. Put the skin strips on a baking tray and briefly cook under a hot grill (broiler) until crisp. Remove and place on paper towel to drain off any fat.

Pull the meat from the duck and tear it into strips, then add it to the bowl with the dressing. Add the mango, watercress, water chestnuts and crispy strips of duck skin. Gently toss together and serve.

seared lamb with almond salad

....

SERVES 4

2 x 300 g (10½ oz) lamb backstraps or
    loin fillets, trimmed
1 tablespoon olive oil

almond salad
50 g (1¾ oz/½ cup) flaked almonds,
    toasted and finely chopped
1 garlic clove, crushed
a handful flat-leaf (Italian) parsley leaves,
    coarsely chopped
10 basil leaves, coarsely chopped
3 ripe roma (plum) tomatoes, finely chopped
¼ red onion, finely diced
3 tablespoons extra virgin olive oil

To make the almond salad, put all of the ingredients in a bowl, season well
with sea salt and freshly ground black pepper and toss to combine. Set aside.

Put the lamb backstraps in a bowl with the olive oil and toss a few times to
thoroughly coat the lamb. Heat a large heavy-based frying pan over high heat.
Add the lamb and sear for 3–5 minutes on each side, or until cooked to your
liking. Transfer to a warm plate, cover loosely with foil and allow to rest for
5 minutes.

Spoon the almond salad into the centre of four serving plates. Slice the
lamb backstraps on the diagonal, arrange the slices over the salad and pour
any meat juices over the top.

The idea for this salad came one day when I was making a chunky tabouleh. I didn't have any cracked wheat and decided to use toasted almonds to create that lovely nuttiness. I knew the result would be lovely with lamb.

There are many theories about where the original Eton mess recipe came from. I have to say that I do love the idea of a hall full of rebellious private school boys creating a classic out of a food fight. However I have to ask why the rebellion, when faced with bowls of berries, cream and meringue?

This is a chewy meringue topped with one of my favourite summer fruit combinations – peaches and passionfruit. The peaches need to be late season and full of flavour. If not, sprinkle them with a little icing sugar before serving.

rose-scented eton mess

SERVES 6

2 egg whites
100 g (3½ oz) caster
  (superfine) sugar
500 g (1 lb 2 oz/3⅓ cups)
  strawberries, hulled and diced
2 teaspoons rosewater
2 tablespoons icing (confectioners')
  sugar, sifted
300 ml (10½ fl oz) thin
  (pouring/whipping) cream,
  whipped

Preheat the oven to 120°C (235°F/Gas ½). Line a baking tray with baking paper.

Using electric beaters, whisk the egg whites until soft peaks form. Add half of the caster sugar and continue to whisk until the mixture is glossy, then add the remaining caster sugar. Continue to whisk until all the sugar has been incorporated.

Spoon dollops of the meringue mixture onto the baking tray to form six meringues and bake in the oven for 1½ hours. Remove the meringues to a wire rack and allow to cool. Store in an airtight container until ready to use.

Put the strawberries, rosewater and icing sugar into a bowl and stir to combine. Set aside to marinate for 10 minutes.

Smash the meringues and layer them in individual bowls with the cream and strawberries, and serve immediately.

summertime pavlova

SERVES 6

3 egg whites
60 g (2 oz/¼ cup) caster
  (superfine) sugar
½ teaspoon white vinegar
¼ teaspoon cream of tartar
1 teaspoon cornflour (cornstarch)
1 teaspoon natural vanilla extract
3 peaches, peeled and thinly sliced
pulp of 3 passionfruit
whipped cream, to serve

Preheat the oven to 150°C (300°F/Gas 2). Line a baking tray with baking paper. Whisk the egg whites until soft peaks form. Gradually add the sugar, then the vinegar, cream of tartar, cornflour and vanilla, and whisk until stiff, glossy peaks form.

Spoon the meringue onto the baking paper to form a 20 cm (8 inch) circle. Bake for 15 minutes, then reduce the oven temperature to 120°C (235°F/Gas ½) and bake for a further 1 hour. Turn the oven off and allow the meringue to cool in the oven with the door slightly ajar.

Serve topped with the peaches, passionfruit and cream.

meringue roulade

SERVES 6

5 egg whites
150 g (5½ oz/⅔ cup) caster (superfine) sugar,
    plus extra, for sprinkling
2 teaspoons cornflour (cornstarch)
1 teaspoon natural vanilla extract
1 teaspoon white vinegar
500 g (1 lb 2 oz/4 cups) raspberries
1 teaspoon orange flower water
200 ml (7 fl oz) thin (pouring/whipping)
    cream, whipped
icing (confectioners') sugar, to serve

Preheat the oven to 160°C (315°F/Gas 2–3). Line a standard baking tray with baking paper.

Whisk the egg whites until soft peaks form, then slowly add the caster sugar and whisk until it has dissolved and the mixture is smooth and glossy. Fold in the cornflour, vanilla and vinegar, then spread the meringue evenly over the baking tray.

Bake for 20 minutes, then remove from the oven and flip over onto a sheet of baking paper sprinkled with a little caster sugar. With the short side facing you, roll the meringue and baking sheet up, like a Swiss roll. Set aside until cool, then unroll.

Put the raspberries into a bowl, sprinkle with the orange flower water and toss until well combined. Spread the whipped cream over the meringue, leaving 3 cm (1¼ inches) clear at one end, and cover with the berries. Carefully roll the meringue up and sprinkle it with icing sugar.

Cut into six thick slices, and serve.

This is such a pretty dessert and the orange flower water adds an extra bit of glamour. You could replace the raspberries with strawberries, blueberries or stewed rhubarb, depending on the season.

This recipe is really all about the peaches but the rosewater brings a little something unexpected to the batter. The filling is rich but light and the browning of the butter is important to the final flavour.

fragrant peach tart

SERVES 8

6–7 small ripe peaches, halved and stones removed
2 eggs
115 g (4 oz/½ cup) caster (superfine) sugar
4 tablespoons plain (all-purpose) flour
½ teaspoon rosewater
110 g (3¾ oz) unsalted butter
thick (double/heavy) cream, to serve

sweet shortcrust tart case
(25 cm/10 inch, with 3 cm/1¼ inch deep sides)
200g (7 oz) plain (all-purpose) flour
100g (3½ oz) unsalted butter, chilled and cut into cubes
1 tablespoon caster (superfine) sugar
2 tablespoons chilled water

Preheat the oven to 180°C (350°F/Gas 4).

To make the shortcrust pastry, put the flour, butter, sugar and a pinch of salt in a food processor and process for 1 minute. Add the chilled water and process until the mixture comes together. Form the pastry into a flat disc and wrap in plastic wrap. Refrigerate for 30 minutes.

Grease a 25 cm tart tin. Roll out the pastry between two sheets of baking paper, then line the tart tin with the pastry. Trim and then chill in the refrigerator for a further 30 minutes.

Line the tart tin with crumpled baking paper and fill with baking beads, uncooked rice or dried beans. Bake for 10–15 minutes, or until the pastry looks golden and dry. Remove and allow to cool.

To make the filling, cut the peaches into thick wedges and arrange, skin side down, on the base of the cooled tart case. Beat the eggs and sugar in a bowl until pale and fluffy. Fold in the flour and rosewater.

Heat the butter in a saucepan over high heat. When it begins to froth and turn pale golden brown, pour it into the egg mixture and beat for 1 minute. Pour the filling over the peaches in the tart case and bake for 35 minutes. Cover the tart with foil and bake for a further 15 minutes, or until the filling has set. Remove from the oven and allow to cool, then cut into slices and serve with the cream.

drunken peaches with raspberry sorbet

SERVES 6

170 g (6 oz/¾ cup) caster (superfine) sugar
300 g (10½ oz/about 2½ cups) frozen raspberries
6 ripe peaches, peeled, halved, stones removed and cut into wedges
750 ml (26 fl oz/3 cups) Prosecco or similar sparkling wine

Put the sugar in a small saucepan with 185 ml (6 fl oz/³⁄₄ cup) water and stir until the sugar has dissolved. Bring to the boil, then reduce the heat and simmer for 2–3 minutes. Remove from the heat and allow the syrup to cool.

To make the raspberry sorbet, put the raspberries and 250 ml (4 fl oz/1 cup) of the sugar syrup in a blender or food processor. Blend to a smooth purée, then strain the liquid through a fine sieve into a bowl. Cover with plastic wrap and freeze for several hours, or overnight.

Put the peaches into six glass coupe bowls or parfait glasses. Pour the Prosecco over, add a scoop of raspberry sorbet and serve immediately.

Yes, it's a little indulgent, but on a hot summer's night you'll thank me when you make this dessert. The sweet tang of the raspberry sorbet is so refreshing and the Prosecco adds fun and bubbles.

I love a dessert that can be made in advance and forgotten about until the final moment. This is quick and easy to make but the honey and cardamom make it feel just a little bit special.

Blood plums seem to come and go quite quickly. Which is a shame, as they really are such a luscious fruit. These are lightly marinated before serving. If you have the time the coconut sorbet is a tropical treat but the plums could also be served with double cream or ice cream.

honey-spiced parfait with fresh berries

SERVES 6

5 egg yolks

100 g (3½ oz) caster (superfine) sugar

2 tablespoons honey

¼ teaspoon ground cardamom

500 ml (17 fl oz/2 cups) crème fraîche or sour cream

fresh raspberries, blackberries or strawberries, to serve

Line an 8 x 22 cm (3¼ x 8½ inch) loaf (bar) tin with baking paper. Set aside.

Using a whisk or electric beaters, whisk the egg yolks, sugar and honey in a large bowl until thick and pale. Gently fold the cardamom and crème fraîche through, then spoon into the prepared tin. Freeze overnight, or until firm.

Cut the parfait into six thick slices and serve with fresh berries.

macerated plums with coconut sorbet

SERVES 6

150 g (5½ oz/⅔ cup) caster (superfine) sugar

1 vanilla bean

250 ml (9 fl oz/1 cup) milk

400 ml (14 fl oz) coconut milk

1 tablespoon golden rum

10 blood plums (about 800 g/ 1 lb 12 oz in total), halved, stones removed and thickly sliced

2 tablespoons dark brown sugar

juice of 1 orange

Put the caster sugar, vanilla bean and 150 ml (5 fl oz) water into a saucepan over medium heat and stir well to dissolve the sugar. Bring the syrup to the boil and let it bubble for 10 minutes. Discard the vanilla bean and pour the syrup into a bowl.

To make the coconut sorbet, pour the milk and coconut milk into the same saucepan over medium heat and let it warm through. Remove the pan from the heat, stir in the vanilla syrup and rum, then allow to cool.

Churn the mixture in an ice-cream machine, or pour it into a shallow container, put it in the freezer, and stir every hour until the sorbet freezes.

Combine the plums, dark brown sugar and orange juice in a bowl and toss until well coated. Cover and refrigerate for 1 hour.

Divide the plums among six bowls and serve with the coconut sorbet.

rum and pineapple ice

SERVES 4

55 g (2 oz/¼ cup) caster (superfine) sugar
500 ml (17 fl oz/2 cups) pineapple juice
1 teaspoon natural vanilla extract
100 ml (3½ fl oz) golden rum
170 ml (5½ fl oz/⅔ cup) coconut milk

Put the sugar and pineapple juice in a saucepan over medium heat. Stir until the sugar has dissolved, then remove from the heat. Stir in the vanilla and rum.

Pour the liquid into a wide shallow container and freeze for 4–5 hours, or until frozen. Remove from the freezer and allow to soften, then break the mixture up using a fork until it looks like crushed ice. Return to the freezer until ready to serve.

Spoon into four chilled glasses and drizzle with the coconut milk.

coffee granita

SERVES 4

1 litre (35 fl oz/4 cups) strong plunger
    or filter coffee
220 g (7¾ oz/1 cup) sugar
6 thick strips of lemon zest
80 ml (2½ fl oz/⅓ cup) Frangelico
    (hazelnut liqueur)
almond bread, to serve

Put the coffee and sugar in a saucepan with the lemon zest strips and bring to the boil. Reduce the heat and allow to simmer for 2–3 minutes, stirring to dissolve the sugar. Remove from the heat and allow to cool.

Stir in the liqueur, then pour into a 20 cm (8 inch) square plastic container. Place in the freezer and leave for 1–2 hours. As crystals start to form, use a large fork to scrape them away from the side of the container and back into the mixture. Repeat every hour for 3–4 hours, or until the granita has frozen into large shards of ice. Return to the freezer until ready to serve.

To serve, scrape the ice with a fork and spoon into four tall chilled glasses. Serve with almond bread.

This recipe was written for a book that had a tropical island as its idyllic setting. Of course we all want to run off to a deserted island at some time or another, and one of my subsequent daydreams resulted in this obvious conclusion — an icy pina colada!

I can remember my first coffee granita because I thought it was the best thing since sliced bread. Sweet icy coffee that dissolved in the mouth and made you want to spring into action. Unfortunately it was late at night and the evening was almost at an end ...

AUTUMN

brunch and lunch

That first chilly morning heralds the end of all that laid back
lusciousness of summer but to be honest that's not such a bad
thing. Suddenly, the style of food that you wish to eat changes
with the cooling air and the lengthening afternoon shadows.
Breakfasts on chilly mornings are more substantial and
lunchtime warrants a bit more warmth. The tones of autumn are
more earthy and rich as the tropical exotica of summer gives
way to the gutsy flavours of garden vegetables. My palate feels
a bit less Asian and a bit more European and that's exciting
because a whole new world of flavours is on the horizon.

baked ricotta with a tomato herb salsa

SERVES 6

600 g (1 lb 5 oz) fresh ricotta cheese
1 teaspoon thyme leaves
10 kalamata olives, pitted and coarsely chopped
2 tablespoons grated parmesan cheese
1 egg, lightly whisked
2 ripe tomatoes, halved, seeds scooped out
    and flesh finely chopped
½ red onion, finely diced
6 large basil leaves, thinly sliced
a handful flat-leaf (Italian) parsley, coarsely chopped
1 teaspoon balsamic vinegar
2 tablespoons extra virgin olive oil
thin slices of sourdough bread, toasted,
    or flat bread, to serveo

Preheat the oven to 180°C (350°F/Gas 4). Line a baking tray with
baking paper.

Put the ricotta in a large bowl with the thyme, olives, parmesan and egg.
Stir to combine. Put a 20 cm (8 inch) spring-form cake tin onto the baking tray
and spoon the ricotta mixture into the tin. Bake for 35–40 minutes, or until
firm and lightly golden. Remove and allow to cool to room temperature.

To make the salsa, put the tomato into a bowl with the onion, basil and
parsley. Add the balsamic vinegar and olive oil and stir until well combined.

Transfer the baked ricotta to a serving plate and spoon the salsa over
the top. Season with sea salt and freshly ground black pepper. Serve
with toasted thin slices of sourdough bread or flat bread.

A simple version of baked ricotta, the tomato salsa brings a light fresh feel to the olive-flecked cheese. Serve with thin toasts or flat bread as part of an antipasti selection, or with a green salad for lunch.

omelette with julienned vegetables

SERVES 2

4 asparagus spears, trimmed and quarterd lengthways
½ small red capsicum (pepper), finely julienned
½ small zucchini (courgette), finely julienned
3 eggs, separated
1 tablespoon butter
12 small basil leaves
30 g (1 oz/⅓ cup, loosely packed) grated
   cheddar cheese

Bring a small saucepan of water to the boil. Add the asparagus spears to the boiling water for 1 minute, then drain and refresh under cold running water. Put the cooked asparagus into a bowl with the capsicum and zucchini.

In a clean bowl, whisk the egg whites until they form soft peaks. Heat the butter in a large non-stick frying pan over medium heat. Fold the egg yolks through the egg whites and pour the mixture into the pan. Cook for 2–3 minutes, or until the base of the omelette is golden brown and firm.

Spread the asparagus, capsicum, zucchini and basil leaves over one side of the omelette and scatter with the cheese. Gently lift up the other side of the omelette and flip it over.

Place the frying pan under a hot grill (broiler) until the omelette is cooked and the cheese is bubbling. Remove from the heat. Divide into two and gently lift onto two serving plates.

A light and healthy brunch for two, this omelette is filled with julienned asparagus, red capsicum and zucchini, and finished with baby basil leaves.

Soft bread soaked in eggy milk and fried until crisp, then drizzled with maple syrup. Some people would think it was a crime to add fresh berries and would be opting instead for crispy bacon. I'll let you decide.

We used to serve a version of this cornbread in a restaurant I worked in years ago. It's a fabulously yummy starting point for a relaxed brunch. Serve it with roast tomatoes, chilli sauce, crisp bacon or an extra dollop of creamy goat's cheese.

cinnamon french toast

SERVES 4

1 egg
1 tablespoon sugar, plus extra,
    for sprinkling
1 teaspoon ground cinnamon
125 ml (4 fl oz/½ cup) milk
butter, for frying
4 thick slices of white bread,
    crusts removed, cut in half
    to make rectangles
fresh seasonal fruit, to serve
100 ml (3½ fl oz) maple syrup,
    to serve
2 tablespoons finely chopped
    toasted pecans, to serve

Whisk the egg, sugar and cinnamon in a bowl. Add the milk and whisk to combine.

Melt the butter in a frying pan over medium heat. Dip the bread into the milk mixture, covering both sides. Sprinkle one side of each piece with the extra sugar and gently fry, sugar side down, for 3 minutes, or until the underside is golden. Sprinkle the tops with a little sugar and flip over. Cook until golden.

Serve with fruit, maple syrup and a sprinkling of pecans.

cornbread

SERVES 6

145 g (5¼ oz/¾ cup) polenta
75 g (2½ oz/½ cup) plain
    (all-purpose) flour
1 tablespoon baking powder
1 tablespoon sugar
1 teaspoon paprika
115 g (4 oz/¾ cup) diced green
    capsicum (pepper)
2 corn cobs, kernels removed
5 spring onions (scallions),
    thinly sliced
30 g (1 oz/1 cup) coriander
    (cilantro) sprigs
3 eggs, lightly whisked
250 ml (9 fl oz/1 cup) buttermilk
170 ml (5½ fl oz/⅔ cup) olive oil
120 g (4¼ oz/1 cup) crumbled
    goat's cheese
½ teaspoon chilli flakes

Preheat the oven to 180°C (350°F/Gas 4). Grease a 20 x 30 cm (8 x 12 inch) baking tin and line it with baking paper.

Combine the polenta, flour, baking powder, sugar and paprika in a bowl. Add the capsicum, corn kernels, spring onions and coriander and mix well. Season with sea salt and freshly ground black pepper.

In a separate bowl, whisk together the eggs, buttermilk and olive oil, then stir the liquid into the dry ingredients. Mix well, then pour the batter into the prepared tin and crumble the goat's cheese over the top. Sprinkle with the chilli flakes. Bake for 35 minutes, or until a skewer inserted into the centre comes out clean.

Cut into six squares and serve with roasted tomatoes and coriander sprigs.

mushroom ragout on brioche

....

SERVES 4

10 g (¼ oz) dried porcini mushrooms
2 tablespoons olive oil
1 onion (preferably brown), diced
2 garlic cloves, finely chopped
2 slices bacon, finely chopped
500 g (1 lb 2 oz) mixed mushrooms, such as Swiss brown,
    shiitake, morels and field, stems removed and thickly sliced
250 ml (9 fl oz/1 cup) red wine
2 tablespoons tomato paste (concentrated purée)
4 thick slices of brioche
1 tablespoon cornflour (cornstarch)
50 g (1¾ oz) shaved pecorino cheese
2 handfuls flat-leaf (Italian) parsley, coarsely chopped

Put the dried porcini mushrooms in a small bowl and cover with 250 ml
(9 fl oz/1 cup) boiling water. Set aside to soak for 15 minutes.

Heat the olive oil in a saucepan over medium heat. Add the onion, garlic
and bacon and cook for 5 minutes, or until the onion is soft and translucent.
Add the fresh mushrooms to the saucepan. Strain the soaking porcini over the
pan so that the soaking liquid drains into it. Finely chop the soaked porcini and
add them to the pan along with the wine, tomato paste and a little sea salt and
freshly ground black pepper. Cover with a lid and simmer for 40 minutes, or
until the mushrooms have cooked and the flavours are well combined.

Toast the brioche. Meanwhile, put the cornflour in a small bowl with
3 tablespoons water and stir until the cornflour has dissolved. Add the
cornflour paste to the mushrooms and stir until the mixture has thickened.

Put the toasted brioche onto four serving plates and top with the mushroom
ragout, some pecorino and a generous scattering of parsley.

Sometimes it's nice to think outside the square for brunch. Autumn is mushroom season and this meal is a celebration of all the varied types you can find at this time of the year. In this recipe I've spooned the mushrooms over brioche and added shaved pecorino but you could also serve them on thick-cut wholemeal bread with a slice of goat's cheese.

Summer has ended but tomatoes are still ripe and plentiful. This is an autumnal approach to tomatoes and a fun way to serve them for breakfast, especially on the weekend, and definitely for Sunday brunch with friends.

By placing the chorizo on top of the tomato and onion, the delicious oils of the sausage ooze down, baking the spicy juices in as the tomato softens. Delicious on toast, these roast tomatoes could also be served with scrambled eggs as part of a big breakfast.

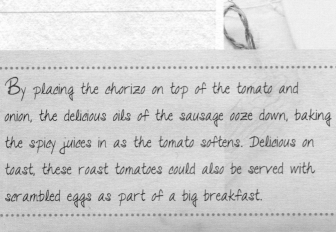

tomatoes with prosciutto, basil and olives

SERVES 4

4 large vine-ripened tomatoes

2 slices of sourdough bread, crusts
    removed, torn into small chunks

8 basil leaves, coarsely torn

12 kalamata olives, pitted and
    coarsely chopped

2 tablespoons finely chopped
    flat-leaf (Italian) parsley

2 tablespoons finely grated
    parmesan cheese

2 tablespoons extra virgin olive oil,
    plus extra, to serve

4 slices of prosciutto

baby basil leaves, for scattering

Preheat the oven to 180°C (350°F/Gas 4). Slice the top from each of the tomatoes. Set the tops aside and, using a small spoon, scoop the flesh and seeds out of the bases and put into a bowl. Add the bread chunks to the bowl along with the basil, olives, parsley, parmesan cheese and olive oil. Stir to combine, then spoon the mixture back into the hollowed-out tomatoes.

Wrap a slice of prosciutto around a tomato, starting at the top, covering the base and returning to the top. Seal with the reserved 'hat' of the tomato, and put into a shallow baking dish. Repeat the process with the remaining three tomatoes.

Bake in the oven for 25–30 minutes. Serve on a plate scattered with baby basil leaves and drizzle over some olive oil.

tomato, onion and chorizo on toast

SERVES 4

4 vine-ripened tomatoes, halved
    crossways

½ red onion, thinly sliced

2 chorizo sausages, thinly sliced

4 slices of thick toast, buttered

a small handful baby cos (romaine)
    lettuce leaves

Preheat the oven to 150°C (300°F/Gas 2).

Put the tomato halves cut side up on a baking tray, season with a little sea salt and top each one with some of the onion slices. Arrange the chorizo slices in a circle on top of the onion.

Bake for 25 minutes, or until the tomatoes are soft and beginning to split.

Serve the tomatoes on toast with baby cos leaves on the side, to garnish.

dill pancakes with smoked salmon

MAKES 24

200 g (7 oz) plain (all-purpose) flour
½ teaspoon salt
2 teaspoons baking powder
2 eggs
250 ml (9 fl oz/1 cup) milk
grated zest of 1 lemon
1 tablespoon finely chopped dill
1 tablespoon butter
1 tablespoon lemon juice
100 g (3½ oz/heaped ⅓ cup) crème fraîche
12 slices of smoked salmon, cut in half
dill sprigs, to serve

To make the pancake batter, sift the flour and salt into a bowl. Stir in the baking powder, then make a well in the centre. In a separate bowl, whisk the eggs and milk together. Pour the liquid ingredients into the dry ingredients and whisk together thoroughly. Stir in the lemon zest and dill. Allow the batter to rest at room temperature for 10 minutes.

Heat a non-stick frying pan over medium heat and grease the surface with a little of the butter. Using 1 tablespoon at a time, drop spoonfuls of batter into the hot pan and cook until the top of the pancake begins to bubble. Flip the pancakes over and cook for a further minute, then remove to a plate, stacking the pancakes to keep them warm. Repeat with the remaining batter; you should have about 24 small pancakes.

Fold the lemon juice through the crème fraîche and season with a little freshly ground black pepper.

Top the pancakes with smoked salmon, a dollop of the lemony crème fraîche, a sprinkle of freshly ground black pepper and a dill sprig to serve.

There's something quite marvellous about the flavour combination of salmon and dill. It's a classic and, for that reason, well worth revisiting. In this recipe, the pancakes are flavoured with lemon and dill, giving them a lovely light flavour.

Jerusalem artichokes are one of those slightly unloved and forgotten vegetables but they make a delicious soup and are also fantastic thrown into the baked vegetable mix for a Sunday roast.

This is a simple and classic soup, teaming chicken with sweet corn. It's perfect for rainy days and lazy Sunday evenings. The cornflour slightly thickens the stock and gives it a lovely texture.

jerusalem artichoke soup

SERVES 4 AS A STARTER OR LIGHT MEAL

1 tablespoon butter
2 onions, diced
500 g (1 lb 2 oz) Jerusalem
  artichokes, peeled and sliced
1 litre (35 fl oz/4 cups) chicken
  stock
100 g (3½ oz) goat's curd
a generous pinch of freshly grated
  nutmeg nutmeg, plus extra,
  to serve

Melt the butter in a saucepan over medium heat. Add the onion and sauté for 5 minutes, or until soft and translucent. Add the Jerusalem artichoke and chicken stock and bring to the boil. Reduce the heat and simmer for 30 minutes, or until the artichoke is soft. Allow to cool.

Purée the soup in a food processor or blender until smooth, then pour it back into the saucepan and gently reheat.

In a small bowl, mix together the goat's curd and nutmeg. Ladle the hot soup into four warmed bowls and add a spoonful of goat's curd to each. Sprinkle with freshly ground black pepper and extra nutmeg.

chicken and corn soup

SERVES 4 AS A STARTER OR LIGHT MEAL

2 tablespoons butter
1 leek, white part only, rinsed
  and finely chopped
2 celery stalks, finely chopped
250 g (9 oz) skinless chicken thigh
  fillets, finely chopped
1 litre (35 fl oz/4 cups) chicken
  stock
3 corn cobs, kernels removed
1 heaped tablespoon cornflour
  (cornstarch)
25 g (1 oz/1 bunch) chives, snipped

Heat a large saucepan over medium heat and add the butter and leek. Sauté for 5 minutes, or until the leek is soft and translucent. Reduce the heat to low and add the celery and chicken. Cover and allow to gently cook for 30 minutes.

Add the stock and corn kernels and bring to the boil. Cook for several minutes, or until the corn has turned golden yellow. Mix the cornflour with 80 ml (2½ fl oz/⅓ cup) water add it to the soup and stir for several minutes.

Ladle the soup into four warmed bowls and sprinkle with the chives.

goat's cheese tart

300 g (10½ oz) soft goat's cheese
3 eggs
5 egg yolks
375 ml (13 fl oz/1½ cups) thin
    (pouring/whipping) cream
25 cm (10 inch) pre-baked
    savoury shortcrust pastry
    case (see recipe below)
mixed leaf salad with walnut oil
    dressing, to serve

walnut oil dressing
1 tablespoon walnut oil
2 tablespoons olive oil
1 tablespoon red wine vinegar
½ teaspoon honey

Preheat the oven to 180°C (350°F/Gas 4). In a food processor, blend the goat's cheese, eggs and egg yolks to a smooth purée. Transfer to a bowl, then fold in the cream. Season with sea salt and freshly ground black pepper.

Put the pastry case (see recipe below) on a baking tray, then pour in the goat's cheese filling. Bake for 30 minutes, or until the top of the tart is lightly golden and the filling is firm. Remove from the oven and allow to cool a little.

When the tart is just warm, serve with a mixed leaf salad and drizzle with the walnut oil dressing.

To make the walnut oil dressing, whisk the ingredients together in a small bowl and season to taste.

savoury shortcrust tart pastry

MAKES 1 LARGE OR 6 SMALL TART CASES

200 g (7 oz/heaped 1⅔ cups)
    plain (all-purpose) flour
100 g (3½ oz) unsalted butter,
    chilled and cut into cubes
2 tablespoons chilled water

Put the flour, butter and a pinch of salt in a food processor and process for 1 minute. Add the chilled water and process until the mixture just comes together. Shape the dough into a disc, wrap in plastic wrap and refrigerate for 30 minutes.

Grease a 25 cm (10 inch) tart tin or six 8 cm (3¼ inch) tartlet tins. Unwrap the pastry and roll it out as thinly as possible between two layers of baking paper, then use the paper to help you line the prepared tin or tins, removing the baking paper once the pastry is in place. Put the tart tin or tins in the refrigerator and chill for a further 30 minutes.

Preheat the oven to 180°C (350°F/Gas 4). Using a fork, prick the pastry case/s over the base, line with baking paper and fill with rice or baking weights. Bake for 10–15 minutes, then remove the baking paper and weights and cook for a further 5 minutes or until the pastry looks cooked and golden. Remove from the oven and allow to cool.

NOTE: *The tart case will keep in the freezer for several weeks, both cooked and uncooked. There is no need to thaw before using—simply put it in the preheated oven directly from the freezer.*

This goat's cheese tart is rich, creamy and velvety in texture and only needs a green salad to complete the picture. Ideally, dress the salad with a walnut oil vinaigrette as the flavours work so well together.

Freshly grated beetroot is such a wonderful ingredient that manages to be both fresh-flavoured and earthy at the same time. Here I've bumped up the earthiness with the toasted sesame seeds and ground coriander, and added an extra layer of freshness with the mint leaves.

beetroot and toasted sesame seed salad

....

SERVES 4 AS A SIDE DISH

50 g (1¾ oz/⅓ cup) sesame seeds
1 tablespoon ground coriander
4 beetroot (beets)
80 ml (2½ fl oz/⅓ cup) balsamic vinegar
80 ml (2½ fl oz/⅓ cup) extra virgin olive oil
a handful mint leaves, coarsely chopped

Put the sesame seeds and ground coriander into a small dry frying pan and cook over medium heat until the sesame seeds are lightly golden. Set aside.

Wearing rubber gloves, peel the beetroot and coarsely grate into a bowl. Add the toasted sesame seeds, balsamic vinegar and olive oil and toss gently to combine. Season to taste with sea salt and freshly ground black pepper.

Spoon the beetroot salad into a serving dish and scatter over the mint.

tofu, broccolini and almonds

SERVES 4

300 g (10½ oz) silken tofu, cut into 2 cm (¾ inch) cubes
235 g (8½ oz/1 bunch) broccolini, halved
2 tablespoons olive oil
2 teaspoons finely grated fresh ginger
2 garlic cloves, crushed
2 tablespoons soy sauce
2 tablespoons mirin
3 large red chillies, seeded and cut into long, thin strips
1 tablespoon butter
50 g (1¾ oz/½ cup) flaked almonds

Put the tofu into a large bowl. Cut the thicker pieces of broccolini in half along the stalk and set aside.

Heat the olive oil in a wok over high heat. Add the ginger and garlic, and as soon as they start to sizzle, add the soy sauce and mirin.

When the sauce begins to bubble, add the broccolini and stir-fry for 2 minutes. Add the chilli and stir-fry for 1 minute, then scoop the vegetables over the tofu in the bowl, leaving the sauce in the wok.

Add the butter to the wok, then the almonds. Stir for 30 seconds, or until the sauce thickly coats the almonds, then spoon the almonds over the tofu and broccolini.

I'm one of those people who actually likes tofu. I can understand the arguments against it (bland and weird texture), but it's for both those reasons that it works for me. True, it needs flavour, but so does bread and pasta and I never hear complaints about those staples. This tofu is brought to life with ginger, garlic, soy sauce and mirin, and then combined with greens and buttery fried almonds. A great salad on its own or served with fish.

One of the simplest of pasta dishes but always a winner. A generous serving of grated parmesan cheese and a drizzle of a robust extra virgin olive oil is all you need.

I know it's very girly but I do love a salad. In the cooler months this doesn't change, but I do want my leafy greens with a bit of extra warmth. This recipe uses cannellini beans for richness and fried chorizo for chilli warmth.

fresh tomato pasta

SERVES 4

4 medium or large, very ripe
  tomatoes, coarsely chopped
1 teaspoon sea salt
2 tablespoons small salted capers,
  rinsed and drained
15 basil leaves, finely chopped
a handful flat-leaf (Italian) parsley,
  coarsely chopped
500 g (1 lb 2 oz) penne pasta
70 g (2½ oz/½ cup) finely grated
  parmesan cheese, plus extra,
  to serve
3 tablespoons olive oil
20 niçoise olives

Put the tomato into a bowl with the sea salt, capers, basil and parsley. Stir gently to coat the tomato, then set aside.

Bring a large saucepan of salted water to the boil and cook the pasta until *al dente*. Drain the pasta, then return to the warm pan. Add the parmesan and olive oil, and stir a few times. Add the tomato, season with freshly ground black pepper and toss to combine.

Divide the pasta among four bowls. Scatter with the olives and the extra parmesan.

chorizo and white bean salad

SERVES 4 AS A STARTER OR LIGHT MEAL

2 tablespoons extra virgin
  olive oil
1 tablespoon red wine
  vinegar
1 teaspoon dijon mustard
400 g (14 oz) tin cannellini
  (white) beans, drained
  and rinsed
250 g (9 oz) cherry
  tomatoes, halved
½ red onion, thinly sliced
2 celery stalks, thinly sliced
a handful flat-leaf (Italian)
  parsley, coarsely
  chopped
250 g (9 oz) chorizo
  sausages, thinly sliced
150 g (5½ oz/1 bunch)
  rocket (arugula), stalks
  trimmed

Put the olive oil, vinegar and mustard in a large bowl and whisk together. Add the beans, cherry tomatoes, onion, celery and parsley and toss lightly to combine.

Heat a non-stick frying pan over medium heat. Sauté the chorizo for 2–3 minutes, or until golden on both sides. Toss the warm chorizo through the salad.

Divide the rocket leaves among four serving plates, then spoon the chorizo salad over the top.

three bean salad with prosciutto

SERVES 4

6 slices prosciutto
175 g (6 oz) green beans
175 g (6 oz) wax beans
    (see Note)
175 g (6 oz) tinned butter beans
2 tablespoons extra virgin olive oil
2 tablespoons white wine vinegar
2 handfuls flat-leaf (Italian) parsley,
    coarsely chopped
2 tablespoons toasted
    pine nuts

Bring a large saucepan of water to the boil.

Meanwhile, grill or pan-fry the prosciutto until it is crisp and then drain on paper towel.

Blanch the green and wax beans in the boiling water for a few minutes or until the green ones begin to turn an emerald green. Drain the beans and briefly refresh them under cold running water.

Return the fresh beans to the saucepan with the butter beans and add the olive oil, vinegar and parsley. Break the prosciutto into small pieces and add it to the beans along with the pine nuts. Toss everything together and season with sea salt and freshly ground black pepper. Pile onto a platter and serve.

NOTE: *Wax beans are similar in taste to green beans and are identified by their yellow colouration. They are usually harvested in late spring and early summer.*

red capsicum, anchovy and egg salad

SERVES 4

4 organic eggs, at room
    temperature
3 red capsicums (peppers)
3 tablespoons extra virgin olive oil
1 teaspoon balsamic vinegar
8 radicchio leaves, torn in half
100 g (3½ oz/3 cups) wild rocket
    (arugula) leaves
1 tablespoon salted capers, rinsed
    and drained
8 good-quality anchovy fillets
1 handful flat-leaf (Italian) parsley

Bring a saucepan of water to the boil, add the eggs and boil for 5 minutes. Remove the eggs from the pan and allow to cool.

Cut the capsicums into large flattish pieces and remove the seeds and membranes. Cook, skin side up, under a hot grill (broiler) until the skin blackens and blisters. Cool in a plastic bag then peel off the skin. Cut or tear the capsicum into long strips and put into a bowl with the olive oil, vinegar and some sea salt and freshly ground black pepper. Toss to coat the capsicum well in the dressing.

Arrange the radicchio leaves on a serving platter, then top with the rocket and dressed capsicum, reserving the marinating mixture in the bowl. Peel the eggs, then cut them in half and add them to the salad. Scatter over the capers, anchovies and parsley. Drizzle with any of the remaining capsicum marinade and serve.

This is a lovely warm autumn salad that has a satisfying richness. As a three-bean salad, it is definitely a culinary step up from the tinned variety!

In this recipe I use white anchovies, which are anchovies that are cured in white vinegar. Their flavour is quite a bit gentler than the more common anchovies, and their texture is a little more fish-like. They are available from most specialty stores and delicatessens. If you can't find them, replace with the common sardine.

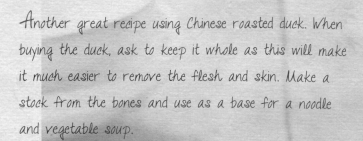

Another great recipe using Chinese roasted duck. When buying the duck, ask to keep it whole as this will make it much easier to remove the flesh and skin. Make a stock from the bones and use as a base for a noodle and vegetable soup.

This is an intensely flavoured tomato sauce, which I've paired with a ricotta–filled ravioli but it could just as easily be spooned over plain penne or orechiette.

duck, fennel and watercress salad

SERVES 4

1 whole Chinese roasted duck
1 large fennel bulb, shaved
4 handfuls picked watercress sprigs
3 tablespoons dry sherry
juice of 1 orange
1 tablespoon soy sauce
1 teaspoon sesame oil
1 teaspoon sugar
1 heaped tablespoon small salted
  capers, rinsed and drained

Preheat the oven to 160°C (315°F/Gas 2–3). Remove the skin from the duck and, using a pair of kitchen scissors, cut the skin into thin strips. Put the strips onto a baking tray and into the oven for 10 minutes, or until the skin starts to become crisp. Remove and drain on paper towel.

Pull the flesh from the duck and roughly shred it. Place the duck flesh and crispy skin into a large bowl and add the shaved fennel and half of the watercress.

In a small bowl, combine the sherry, orange juice, soy sauce, sesame oil and sugar. Stir until the sugar has dissolved, then drizzle over the salad. Arrange the remaining watercress on a serving platter or in a bowl and top with the duck salad. Toss lightly, then scatter over the capers.

ricotta ravioli with tomato sauce

SERVES 4

5 vine-ripened tomatoes
4 spring onions (scallions),
  thinly sliced
1 tablespoon small salted capers,
  rinsed and drained
100 ml (3½ fl oz) extra virgin
  olive oil
600 g (1 lb 5 oz) fresh ricotta
  ravioli
40 g (1½ oz/⅓ cup) coarsely
  grated parmesan cheese
20 small black olives

Bring a large saucepan of water to the boil. Cut an X-shape in the base of each of the tomatoes, then drop them into the boiling water for a minute. Scoop them out and peel away the skin, then cut the tomatoes into quarters. Using a sharp knife, remove and discard the seeds from the tomatoes.

Thinly slice the tomato flesh into long strips and put into a saucepan with the spring onion, capers and olive oil. Simmer over low heat for 5 minutes.

Bring a saucepan of salted water to the boil and cook the ravioli until *al dente*. Drain and divide among four pasta bowls. Spoon the warm tomato sauce over the ravioli and scatter over the parmesan cheese and olives.

beetroot salad with labne

SERVES 4 AS A SIDE DISH

200 g (7 oz/¾ cup) Greek-style yoghurt
   (to make labne)
4 beetroot (beets)
2 tablespoons olive oil
1 tablespoon sumac
1 tablespoon lemon thyme leaves
a large handful coarsely chopped
   flat-leaf (Italian) parsley
25 g (1 oz/1 bunch) chives, snipped
juice of 1 lemon

To make the labne, put the yoghurt into a muslin-lined seive over a bowl. Refrigerate overnight but do not cover. Remove the thickened yoghurt in heaped tablespoonfuls and roll into balls. (If not using straight away, marinate the yoghurt balls in olive oil flavoured with spices, garlic and lemon zest.)

Preheat the oven to 200°C (400°F/Gas 6).

Wearing rubber gloves, peel the beetroot and cut into bite-sized chunks. Put the beetroot, olive oil, sumac and lemon thyme into a bowl and toss to coat the beetroot. Transfer the beetroot to a roasting tin and cover with a lid or foil. Bake for 30 minutes, or until the beetroot is cooked through. Remove and set aside to cool.

Put the beetroot into a bowl with the herbs and lemon juice and toss well. Spoon into a serving bowl and top with spoonfuls of the labne.

fig and goat's cheese salad

SERVES 4 AS A STARTER

1 teaspoon wildflower honey
1 teaspoon balsamic vinegar
1 teaspoon wholegrain mustard
3 teaspoons extra virgin olive oil
6 slices of prosciutto
6 large figs, thinly sliced
100 g (3½ oz/3 cups) wild rocket (arugula) leaves
100 g (3½ oz) goat's cheese, cut into 4 rounds

Combine the honey, vinegar, mustard and olive oil in a large bowl.

Heat a non-stick frying pan over medium heat and cook the prosciutto until crisp and golden. Remove from the pan and drain on paper towel.

Arrange the figs on four serving plates. Stir the dressing again, then add the rocket and toss lightly. Crumble over the prosciutto and toss again before piling the salad onto the sliced figs. Top each salad with a slice of goat's cheese.

I know it's a bit of a bother but making your own labne is so much fun. I always feel like a proud cheese-maker, which is one of my dream occupations, by the way. But don't panic, nowadays labne is available at most delicatessens and cheese counters. This is a lovely autumn salad of creamy cheese and beetroot.

Fresh figs and goat's cheese is a combination made in heaven. This is one of those recipes that is more about the shopping than the cooking. The figs need to be beautifully ripe and the prosciutto wafer thin.

Roast pumpkin is a favourite of mine from childhood. It has to be cooked to a gooey richness and if a little burnt then all the better. When combined with lentils and goat's cheese it becomes a hearty salad that will make any vegetarian or vegetable-lover smile.

Here comes another of my fresh-and-easy pasta sauces. This one combines the classic flavours of tomato, tuna, capers, olives, basil and rocket. Super simple and super yummy.

lentil and pumpkin salad

SERVES 4

1 kg (2 lb 4 oz) jap or kent pumpkin (winter squash),
    peeled, seeds removed and cut into bite-sized chunks
1 large red onion, halved and thinly sliced
2 tablespoons olive oil
120 g (4¼ oz) puy lentils or tiny blue-green lentils
½ teaspoon sea salt
1 teaspoon wholegrain mustard
1 tablespoon balsamic vinegar
2 tablespoons extra virgin olive oil
a handful flat-leaf (Italian) parsley, coarsely chopped
50 g (1¾ oz/1½ cups) wild rocket (arugula) leaves
100 g (3½ oz) goat's cheese

Preheat the oven to 180°C (350°F/Gas 4).

Put the pumpkin onto a baking tray and scatter over the onion. Drizzle with the olive oil and season with a little sea salt and freshly ground black pepper. Bake for 25 minutes, or until the pumpkin is cooked through and the onion is starting to blacken a little on the ends.

Meanwhile, put the lentils in a small saucepan with the sea salt and 500 ml (17 fl oz/2 cups) water. Bring to the boil, then simmer for 30 minutes, or until tender. Drain the lentils and stir in the mustard, vinegar, extra virgin olive oil and parsley.

Arrange the rocket leaves on a serving plate, top with the pumpkin and onion, then spoon over the lentils. Crumble the goat's cheese over the top and serve.

casareccia with tuna and tomato

SERVES 4

400 g (14 oz) casareccia or penne pasta
185 g (6½ oz) tinned tuna in oil, drained
3 ripe tomatoes, coarsely chopped
3 tablespoons extra virgin olive oil
1 tablespoon small salted capers, rinsed and drained
12 olives, pitted and coarsely chopped
10 basil leaves, roughly torn
150 g (5½ oz) coarsely chopped rocket (arugula) leaves
70 g (2½ oz) shaved parmesan cheese, to serve

Bring a large saucepan of salted water to the boil. Cook the pasta until *al dente*. Meanwhile, coarsely flake the tuna into a large bowl. Add the tomato, olive oil, capers, olives, basil and rocket.

Drain the cooked pasta and add it to the bowl. Toss to combine the ingredients well, then divide among four warmed pasta bowls. Top with the parmesan cheese and serve.

linguine with prawns and fresh herbs

SERVES 4

400 g (14 oz) linguine
100 ml (3½ fl oz) light olive oil
3 garlic cloves, finely chopped
20 raw king prawns (shrimp), peeled and deveined, tails left intact
250 g (9 oz) cherry tomatoes, halved
a handful flat-leaf (Italian) parsley leaves
12 basil leaves
2 tablespoons snipped chives
juice of 1 lemon

Bring a large saucepan of salted water to the boil and cook the linguine until *al dente*. Drain and return it to the warm saucepan.

Heat the olive oil in a frying pan over medium heat and add the garlic, stirring briefly before adding the prawns. Cook the prawns until they are pink on both sides and beginning to curl. Add the tomatoes and cook for a further minute. Remove from the heat.

Add the prawn mixture, all the herbs and the lemon juice to the pasta. Season with sea salt and freshly ground black pepper and toss. Serve in four pasta bowls.

fig, apple and gorgonzola salad

SERVES 4

1 teaspoon lemon juice
2 tablespoons extra virgin olive oil
100 g (3½ oz/2¼ cups) baby rocket (arugula) leaves
4 figs, quartered
1 pink lady apple, thinly sliced
100 g (3½ oz) gorgonzola cheese

Put the lemon juice and olive oil into a small bowl and stir to combine. Season lightly with sea salt and freshly ground black pepper.

Divide the rocket among four serving plates. Arrange the fig and apple pieces on top of the rocket, then crumble the gorgonzola over the salad. Spoon the dressing over the top.

This is such a simple combination of flavours but it's a firm favourite with many people. A slightly indulgent midweek meal that's easy to whip up.

With its rich cream and mouldy tang, gorgonzola is a polarising ingredient. However, for those who love it, here's a great salad of apple, fig, rocket and crumbled cheese.

I love a fish cake. There is something homely and comforting about them, even a little old fashioned, but add a great mayonnaise or chilli sauce and they are suddenly a meal worth taking notice of. They also make the perfect Sunday night TV dinner.

salt and pepper crab cakes

MAKES 12

4 thick slices of sourdough bread,
    torn into small pieces
300 g (10½ oz) fresh crabmeat
½ teaspoon oregano leaves
a handful flat-leaf (Italian) parsley,
    coarsely chopped
2 spring onions (scallions), thinly sliced
½ teaspoon white pepper
3 eggs, whisked
vegetable oil, for frying
lemon cheeks, to serve
wilted English spinach leaves, to serve

lemon mayonnaise
2 egg yolks
1 teaspoon mustard
1 tablespoon lemon juice
200 ml (7 fl oz) light olive oil

Preheat the oven to 130°C (250°F/Gas 1).

To make the lemon mayonnaise, whisk together the egg yolks, mustard and lemon juice until light and creamy. Drizzle in the olive oil, a little at a time, whisking continuously until a thick mayonnaise forms. Season to taste. This will make about 235 g (8½ oz/1 cup). (The mayonnaise will keep for 2 weeks in the refrigerator.)

Put the bread into the food processor or blender and process to form coarse breadcrumbs. Put them into a large bowl and add the crabmeat, oregano, parsley, spring onion and white pepper. Season generously with sea salt, then toss until well combined. Stir in the egg. Form the mixture into 12 round cakes and put them on a tray.

Pour the oil into a frying pan to fill it to 5 mm (¼ inch). Heat over medium heat. When the surface of the oil begins to shimmer, cook the crab cakes, a few at a time, for 2–3 minutes, or until deep golden on both sides. Drain on paper towel and put them onto a baking tray and keep in the oven while cooking the remaining crab cakes.

Serve with wilted spinach, lemon cheeks and a bowl of lemon mayonnaise.

saffron, tomato and chicken risotto

SERVES 4

1 litre (35 fl oz/4 cups) chicken stock
a generous pinch of saffron threads
2 tablespoons butter
2 garlic cloves, finely chopped
1 leek, white part only, rinsed and thinly sliced
330 g (11½ oz/1½ cups) risotto rice
125 ml (4 fl oz/½ cup) white wine
300 g (10½ oz) skinless chicken thigh fillets, diced
3 ripe roma (plum) tomatoes, diced
1 tablespoon finely grated lemon zest
4 tablespoons grated parmesan cheese
baby rocket (arugula) leaves, to serve
extra virgin olive oil, to serve

Bring the chicken stock to the boil in a saucepan, then reduce the heat and keep at a low simmer. Put the saffron threads into a cup and cover with 125 ml (4 fl oz/½ cup) hot water.

Heat a large saucepan over medium heat. Add the butter, garlic and leek and sauté for 5 minutes, or until the leek is soft. Add the rice and stir for 1 minute, or until it is well coated and the grains are glossy. Stir once more, then add the wine.

Ladle 250 ml (9 fl oz/1 cup) of the hot stock into the pan and simmer, stirring occasionally until it has been completely absorbed. Add another 250 ml stock, the chicken, tomato and saffron liquid. Stir for 2–3 minutes, until the stock is completely absorbed, then add another 250 ml of the stock. Cook, stirring occasionally, until all of the liquid has been absorbed, then test the rice to see if it is *al dente*. If it needs more cooking, stir in the remaining stock.

Fold the lemon zest and half of the parmesan through the risotto. Spoon into four warmed pasta bowls and sprinkle with the remaining parmesan. Scatter over a few rocket leaves and drizzle with a little olive oil.

A deeply comforting bowl of soupy rice, flavoured with chicken and saffron. This is one for those nights when you feel a bit run down and sorry for yourself. Under such circumstances it should be eaten while you're curled up in a deeply cushioned sofa watching re-runs of a BBC historical drama.

This is a filling side salad to serve alongside spicy roast chicken or lamb. The corn is sautéed with paprika, oregano and chilli, giving it a lovely bite, which is well matched by the nuttiness of the burghul.

I used to make this salad every day for several years. It was a well-loved menu item and was rarely not on offer. Of course it's really perfect autumn food as the main flavours are pear and walnut. The walnut dressing has a touch of orange to give it zing and needs a generous amount of seasoning to make the walnuts sing.

tomato, corn and burghul salad

SERVES 4 AS A SIDE DISH OR LIGHT MEAL

2 vine-ripened tomatoes, diced
60 g (2¼ oz/⅓ cup) burghul
    (bulgur)
2 tablespoons olive oil
1 red onion, thinly sliced
½ teaspoon smoked paprika
½ teaspoon dried oregano
1 large red chilli, seeded and
    finely chopped
2 corn cobs, kernels removed
a handful coriander (cilantro) leaves

Put the tomato in a large bowl. Sprinkle generously with sea salt and set aside.

Put the burghul in a bowl and add 150 ml (5 fl oz) cold water. Cover with plastic wrap and set aside for 10 minutes to allow the grains to absorb the water.

Meanwhile, heat the olive oil in a deep-sided frying pan over medium heat. Add the onion and sauté for 5 minutes, or until it becomes soft and translucent. Add the paprika, oregano, chilli and corn kernels and cook for a further 2–3 minutes, or until all the corn has turned a deep golden colour. Remove from the heat. Squeeze any excess liquid from the burghul, then add to the tomato with the corn mixture. Toss to combine, then fold through the coriander leaves.

pear and walnut salad

SERVES 4

115 g (4 oz/1 cup) walnut halves
½ garlic clove
1 teaspoon sea salt
juice and grated zest of 1 orange
125 ml (4 fl oz/½ cup) light olive oil
4 beurre bosc pears, thinly sliced
100 g (3½ oz) lamb's lettuce
    (corn salad)
140 g (5 oz) goat's curd

Put the walnuts, garlic, sea salt, orange zest and olive oil into a blender or food processor and process to form a thick sauce.

Put the orange juice into a bowl and add the pear. Season with freshly ground black pepper. Add the lamb's lettuce and toss lightly to combine.

Divide the salad among four serving plates and spoon the goat's curd on top. Drizzle the salad with any remaining orange juice, then spoon the walnut dressing over the goat's curd.

Smoky baked eggplant is one of those great culinary inventions for which we must all give thanks. If you're not an eggplant fan, then you won't know what I'm talking about, but for those who are, here's a lovely salad.

crushed eggplant and tomato salad

SERVES 4 AS A SIDE DISH

4 roma (plum) tomatoes, diced
1 teaspoon sugar
1 teaspoon ground cumin
1 large eggplant (aubergine)
1 tablespoon balsamic vinegar
2 tablespoons extra virgin olive oil, plus extra for brushing
a handful chopped flat-leaf (Italian) parsley
10 mint leaves, finely chopped
2 spring onions (scallions), thinly sliced

Put the tomato in a large bowl, sprinkle with the sugar and cumin and season generously with sea salt and freshly ground black pepper. Set aside.

To prepare the eggplant, prick it all over with a skewer and then sit it directly on a naked flame of a gas burner or barbecue. Set the flames to low–medium and cook for 10 minutes, turning the eggplant occasionally until it is blackened and blistered and beginning to collapse. (If you don't have a gas stove, lightly rub the eggplant in oil, then bake in a preheated oven at 200°C (400°F/Gas 6) until it is cooked through—it will begin to collapse inwards and will feel soft and mushy when pressed with a finger.) Place the eggplant in a bowl and cover with plastic wrap. Allow to cool.

Peel the charred skin from the eggplant. Put the eggplant in a colander over a bowl, then cut or tear into long strips. Using your hands, press down on the eggplant to remove the excess liquid.

Add the eggplant to the tomato along with the vinegar, olive oil, parsley, mint and spring onion. Season to taste with sea salt and freshly ground black pepper and gently mix together.

coriander and pine nut lentils

SERVES 4

150 g (5½ oz) puy lentils
3 teaspoons sea salt
120 g (4¼ oz) cracked wheat
60 g (2¼ oz) currants
60 g (2¼ oz) butter
1 large red onion, diced
2 carrots, diced
2 teaspoons ras al hanout (see Note)
150 ml (5 fl oz) chicken stock
2 handfuls coriander (cilantro) leaves
a handful flat-leaf (Italian) parsley leaves
60 g (2¼ oz) pine nuts, toasted

Put the lentils into a saucepan with the sea salt, cover with 500 ml
(17 fl oz/2 cups) water, and bring to the boil over high heat. Reduce the
heat to medium and simmer for 35 minutes. Drain and set aside.

Put the cracked wheat and currants into a bowl and cover with boiling
water. Allow them to absorb the water.

Put the butter into a large heavy-based saucepan and heat over medium
heat. Add the onion and carrot and cook until the onion is soft and golden.
Add the ras al hanout, lentils, cracked wheat, currants and chicken stock.
Stir well, cover, reduce the heat to low and simmer for 5 minutes.

Spoon the lentil mixture into a large serving dish. Sprinkle with the
herbs and pine nuts.

NOTE: *Ras al hanout is a classic spice blend used in Moroccan cooking. The
name means 'top of the shop' or the very best spice blend that a spice merchant
has to offer. It contains a varied selection of spices, including paprika, cumin,
ginger, coriander seed, allspice, cardamom and nutmeg. It is available from the
spice section of most large supermarkets.*

I love a lentil dish, and the idea for this salad
came when I went to a restaurant that served
an amazing side dish of baked mixed grains.
It inspired me to think about ways to use various
grainy combinations — like this.

AUTUMN

FIGS

warm plates

I always think autumn is an interesting season because no sooner do we see the leaves starting to turn golden brown and drift from the branches than all the food becomes suddenly earthy and reminiscent of woodlands. And just as a healthy jaunt through the woods requires at this time an extra layer to offset the new chill in the air, so too does the food become warmer and more comforting. It's the time of the year to delight in figs, pumpkins, pears, mushrooms, plums and dark leafy greens. Time to explore spices and heavy seasonings, revisit old grainy favourites and enjoy some richer flavours and more substantial dinners.

lamb cutlets with smoky eggplant

SERVES 4

1 large eggplant (aubergine)
3 tablespoons plain Greek-style yoghurt
½ teaspoon ground cumin
½ garlic clove
250 g (9 oz) cherry tomatoes, quartered
6 bottled artichoke hearts, drained and cut into wedges
a handful flat-leaf (Italian) parsley
12 lamb cutlets, French-trimmed

To prepare the eggplant, prick it all over with a skewer and then sit it directly on a naked flame of a gas burner or barbecue. Set the flames to low–medium and cook for 10 minutes, turning the eggplant occasionally until it is blackened and blistered and beginning to collapse. (If you don't have a gas stove, lightly rub the eggplant in oil, then bake in a preheated oven at 200°C (400°F/Gas 6) until it is cooked through—it will begin to collapse inwards and will feel soft and mushy when pressed with a finger.) Place the eggplant in a bowl and cover with plastic wrap. Allow to cool.

Peel the charred skin from the eggplant and put the flesh in a colander over a bowl. Using a pair of kitchen scissors, roughly cut the flesh into small pieces. Using your hands, press down on the eggplant to remove excess liquid. Put the eggplant into a food processor with the yoghurt, cumin and garlic, and purée. Season to taste with sea salt and freshly ground black pepper.

Put the tomato, artichoke and parsley in a bowl. Toss to combine. Set aside.

Heat a large non-stick frying pan or chargrill pan over high heat. Add the lamb cutlets and sear for 2–3 minutes on each side. Transfer to a warm plate, cover loosely with foil and allow to rest for 5 minutes.

Spoon the eggplant purée onto four plates and put the lamb cutlets on top. Add any lamb juices to the tomato salad, toss, then pile beside the cutlets.

The smoky eggplant accompaniment teams beautifully with the lamb cutlets, while the vinegary artichoke salad adds a lovely bite and freshness.

Sometimes I think Asian soups are, visually, like small rock pools. You want to dip in and see what strange creatures are lurking beneath the surface. No strange creatures here, but a simple shiitake-flavoured broth with capsicum and tofu.

simmered vegetables and tofu

SERVES 4

1 garlic clove, thinly sliced
2 tablespoons soy sauce
2 teaspoons sesame oil
125 ml (4 fl oz/½ cup) shaoxing rice wine
125 ml (4 fl oz/½ cup) mirin
2 star anise
1 tablespoon thinly sliced fresh ginger
12 fresh shiitake mushrooms, halved if large
1 red capsicum (pepper), cut into 1 cm (½ inch) pieces
1 yellow capsicum (pepper), cut into 1 cm (½ inch) pieces
300 g (10½ oz) silken tofu, cut into 1.5 cm (⅝ inch) cubes
2 spring onions (scallions), thinly sliced on the diagonal
steamed white or brown rice, to serve

Put the garlic, soy sauce, sesame oil, rice wine, mirin, star anise, ginger, mushrooms and capsicum in a large saucepan. Add 500 ml (12 fl oz/2 cups) water and bring to the boil over high heat. Reduce the heat to low and simmer for 10 minutes.

Divide the tofu among four warmed bowls. Spoon the vegetables and broth over the top. Garnish with the spring onion and serve with rice.

lamb backstraps with puy lentils, broad beans and feta

SERVES 4

150 g (5½ oz) puy lentils or tiny blue-green lentils
2 tablespoons lemon juice
2 tablespoons olive oil
255 g (9 oz/1⅔ cups) frozen broad (fava) beans
2 lamb backstraps or loin fillets (about 500 g/
    1 lb 2 oz in total), trimmed
150 g (5½ oz) feta cheese
10 mint leaves, torn

Put the lentils in a saucepan and cover with 500 ml (17 fl oz/2 cups) water. Bring to the boil and simmer for 30 minutes, or until the lentils are soft. Drain and place in a bowl with the lemon juice and olive oil. Season with sea salt and freshly ground black pepper.

Bring a saucepan of salted water to the boil and add the broad beans. Cook for 5 minutes, then drain and rinse under cold running water. Peel away the outer layer of the pods, then stir the broad beans through the lentils.

Heat a large heavy-based frying pan over high heat. Add the lamb and sear until the uncooked side begins to look a little bloody. Turn the lamb over, reduce the heat and cook for a further 5 minutes. Transfer to a warm plate, cover loosely with foil and allow to rest for 5 minutes.

Crumble the feta into the lentils. Add the mint. Thickly slice the lamb across the grain and add any meat juices to the lentils. Lightly toss the lentil salad, then spoon onto four plates and top with the warm lamb slices.

Years ago, when I was still at school, I went to a Greek barbecue. They served spit-roasted lamb, drenched in lemon juice, which was a revelation after years of greasy grilled lamb chops (sorry, Mum). This combination of lentils, broad beans and goat's cheese with seared lamb needs a squeeze of lemon to bring all the flavours together.

Some people seem to be scared of risotto, believing that you have to treat them with great dedication or it will all go horribly wrong. However I've found a healthy disregard works wonders. Yes, you have to stir them, but so what? You just have to get a nice 'feel' for risotto. If you do, the rewards are great because this dish is one of the simplest midweek meals and can be made out of the most humble of ingredients.

tomato and prosciutto risotto

SERVES 4

1 litre (35 fl oz/4 cups) chicken or vegetable stock
4 large slices of prosciutto, halved crossways
2 tablespoons butter
2 garlic cloves, finely chopped
2 leeks, white part only, rinsed and thinly sliced
330 g (11½ oz/1½ cups) risotto rice
3 ripe roma (plum) tomatoes, diced
2 tablespoons dry sherry
4 tablespoons grated parmesan cheese
extra virgin olive oil, to serve
rocket (arugula) or basil, to serve

Bring the stock to the boil in a saucepan, then reduce the heat and keep at a low simmer.

Heat a large saucepan over medium heat. Add the prosciutto and cook on both sides until golden and crisp, then remove and drain on paper towel. Add the butter, garlic and leek to the pan and sauté for 4–5 minutes, or until the leek is soft and translucent. Add the rice and stir for 1 minute, or until the rice is well coated and the grains are glossy.

Ladle 250 ml (9 fl oz/1 cup) of the hot stock into the pan and simmer, stirring occasionally, until it has been completely absorbed. Add another 250 ml of the stock and the tomato. Cook, stirring, for a further few minutes until the stock has been completely absorbed, then add another 250 ml of the stock. Cook, stirring occasionally, until all of the liquid has been absorbed, then test the rice to see if it is *al dente*. If it needs more cooking, add the remaining stock. Splash in the sherry, then lightly fold half of the parmesan through.

Spoon into four warmed pasta bowls and sprinkle with the remaining parmesan. Crumble the prosciutto into smaller pieces and scatter over the risotto. Drizzle with a little olive oil and garnish with rocket or basil.

roast pumpkin and tofu salad

SERVES 4–6

700 g (1 lb 9 oz) jap or kent
    pumpkin (winter
    squash), peeled
2 tablespoons olive oil
grated zest and juice of 1 lime
1 tablespoon fish sauce
1 tablespoon soy sauce
100 ml (3½ fl oz) mirin
400 g (14 oz) broccolini, trimmed
200 g (7 oz) firm tofu, cut into
    2 cm (¾ inch) cubes
1 tablespoon sesame seeds, toasted

Preheat the oven to 180°C (350°F/Gas 4).

Cut the pumpkin into bite-sized pieces and put them into a large bowl. Add the olive oil and season with sea salt and freshly ground black pepper. Toss until the pumpkin is well coated and transfer to a roasting tin. Roast for 20 minutes, or until golden brown and tender.

To make the dressing, put the lime zest, lime juice, fish sauce, soy sauce and mirin in a large non-metallic bowl and stir.

Bring a saucepan of water to the boil. Add the broccolini and cook for 2 minutes, or until just tender. Drain.

Add the broccolini, pumpkin, tofu and sesame seeds to the bowl with the dressing. Gently toss and serve.

goat's cheese omelette

SERVES 2

3 eggs, separated
1 tablespoon butter
1 teaspoon finely snipped chives
50 g (1¾ oz) goat's cheese,
    crumbled
buttered toast and rocket
    (arugula) leaves, to serve

Whisk the egg whites into soft peaks. In a separate bowl, lightly whisk the egg yolks, then gently fold them into the egg whites.

Heat a 25 cm (10 inch) non-stick frying pan over high heat and add the butter. When the butter has melted and begins to sizzle, pour in the egg mixture. Using a spatula, fold the edges of the egg into the centre as it cooks. When the egg is nearly cooked, sprinkle with the chives and goat's cheese. Flip one half of the omelette over the other and take the pan off the heat.

Divide the omelette between two plates and serve with buttered toast and rocket leaves.

The salty sweet dressing used on this salad works beautifully with the roast pumpkin and sesame seeds. Because of the flavour combination, this salad would work best with chicken or seafood.

It's an old theory but still very much true that everyone should master a version of the classic omelette – the perfect breakfast, lunch or supper dish when time is limited, the refrigerator is empty or you want something that says 'home'.

I think everyone loves a chicken pho. And while it always tastes great in a busy restaurant with sticky formica tables, it's also a soup for quiet nights at home when the winning combination of soupy smooth stock and zingy herbs and chilli can be enjoyed in peace.

chicken pho

225 g (8 oz) dried rice stick noodles
1.5 litres (52 fl oz/6 cups) good-quality chicken stock
2 free-range skinless chicken breast fillets,
    thinly sliced against the grain
a handful mint leaves
a handful coriander (cilantro) leaves
a handful holy basil leaves
100 g (3½ oz) mung bean sprouts
2 red chillies, seeded and thinly sliced
80 g (2¾ oz/½ cup) Asian fried shallots
    (see Note on page 109)
1 lime, quartered
fish sauce, to serve

Place the rice stick noodles in a large bowl, cover with warm water and allow them to soak for 30 minutes, or until they are soft.

Place the chicken stock in a saucepan over medium heat and bring to a soft rolling boil. Reduce the heat.

Fill another large saucepan with water and bring it to the boil. Divide the soaked rice stick noodles into four batches and cook each batch separately, for about 10 seconds, lowering it into the boiling water with a sieve.

Put the rice stick noodles into four bowls. Put the chicken into the sieve and cook in the boiling water for 2 minutes.

Put the chicken into the four bowls and top with the stock. Garnish with the herbs, mung bean sprouts, chilli and fried shallots. Serve with the lime and fish sauce as extra seasoning.

pappardelle with basil, feta and roast capsicum

SERVES 4

4 red capsicums (peppers)
3 tablespoons extra virgin olive oil
1 teaspoon balsamic vinegar
120 g (4¼ oz) basil
400 g (14 oz) pappardelle
150 g (5½ oz) feta cheese

Preheat the oven to 200°C (400°F/Gas 6).

Rub the capsicums with a little of the olive oil, slice them in half lengthways and put them in a roasting tin skin side up. Bake for 20 minutes, or until the skin blackens and blisters. Put the capsicums in a plastic bag, allow them to cool and remove the skin and seeds. Put the flesh of the capsicum, the balsamic vinegar and 10 of the basil leaves in a blender. Season with sea salt and freshly ground black pepper and blend.

Add the strained liquid from the roasting tin and a little of the olive oil to give the capsicum a saucy consistency. Put the sauce in a large saucepan over low heat to keep it warm.

Cook the pappardelle until it is *al dente*, then drain the pasta and add it to the warm capsicum sauce. Crumble half of the feta through the pasta and toss. Serve garnished with the remaining basil leaves and the rest of the feta crumbled on top.

Tamarind gives food a lovely sweet-sour flavour and is used in various cuisines around the world. These prawns have a wonderful hot, spicy, sour, sweet flavour, which is softened with a drizzle of coconut milk and the steamed rice.

sweet and sour prawns

SERVES 4

½ teaspoon cayenne pepper
1 teaspoon ground turmeric
1 tablespoon tamarind purée (see Note on page 79)
20 raw king prawns (shrimp), peeled
    and deveined, tails left intact
2 tablespoons vegetable oil
2 red onions, thinly sliced
1 red capsicum (pepper), cut into 1 cm (½ inch) pieces
1 tablespoon grated palm sugar (jaggery) or soft brown sugar
1 tablespoon balsamic vinegar
steamed white rice, to serve
100 ml (3½ fl oz) coconut milk
a handful coriander (cilantro) sprigs

Put the cayenne pepper, turmeric and tamarind purée in a non-metallic bowl and stir to combine. Add the prawns and toss until well coated. Cover and refrigerate until ready to cook.

Put the oil in a large heavy-based frying pan over low–medium heat. Add the onion and cook for 20 minutes, stirring occasionally, until the onion is soft and beginning to caramelise. Add the capsicum, sugar and vinegar and cook for a further 2 minutes.

Add the prawns, laying them on their sides in a single layer over the onion mixture, and cook for 1½–2 minutes on each side, or until they are starting to curl up and turn pink; you may need to cook the prawns in two batches if your pan isn't quite large enough to fit them all at once.

Serve the prawns and sauce on top of steamed white rice, drizzled with the coconut milk and scattered with the coriander sprigs.

spiced duck breast

4 duck breast fillets, skin on
2 tablespoons brown sugar
½ teaspoon Sichuan peppercorns
1 star anise
1 tablespoon sea salt
125 ml (4 fl oz/½ cup) brandy
4 dried shiitake mushrooms
2 thin leeks, rinsed and cut into short lengths
400 g (14 oz) jap or butternut pumpkin (winter squash),
    peeled and cut into cubes
2 tablespoons light olive oil

Preheat the oven to 180°C (350°F/Gas 4). Score the skin of the duck in a crisscross pattern. Put the brown sugar, peppercorns and star anise into a spice grinder (or use a mortar and pestle) with the sea salt and grind them together. Rub this mixture into the duck skin. Put the brandy in a small container, add the duck breasts, skin side up, cover and marinate for at least 1 hour or overnight.

Soak the dried mushrooms in 500 ml (17 fl oz/2 cups) boiling water for 30 minutes. Strain the liquid into a baking dish and thinly slice the mushrooms. Put the mushroom into the baking dish with the leeks and pumpkin, season, cover with foil and bake for 30 minutes, or until the pumpkin is soft. Increase the heat to 200°C (400°F/Gas 6).

Heat a frying pan over high heat and sear the duck, skin side down, until it is lightly browned. Put the duck breasts onto a wire rack set over a baking tray, this time skin side up, and drizzle them with the brandy marinade. Roast them for 15 minutes. (If the duck skin hasn't completely crisped up in your oven, place the skin under a hot grill for 1 minute.) Arrange the pumpkin and leek on four warmed plates and top with a thinly sliced duck breast.

There is something about the skin of the duck that just cries out for sugar and salt. These duck breasts have a mixture of sugar, salt, Sichuan peppercorns and star anise rubbed into them. A wonderful combination that smells of the spice shelves in Chinatown.

Mmmm yum ... pork belly. Possibly not a dish to eat every night, but with all that velvety richness, who can resist the odd chance to pig out. The green mango salad does allay some of the guilt by bringing a nice fresh bite to the dish.

pork belly with green mango salad

SERVES 4

1 kg (2 lb 4 oz) piece of pork belly
150 ml (5 fl oz) light soy sauce
80 ml (2½ fl oz/⅓ cup) Chinese rice wine or sherry
500 ml (17 fl oz/2 cups) salt-reduced chicken stock
1½ teaspoons Chinese five-spice
2 short red chillies, halved lengthways and seeded
1 cinnamon stick
4 star anise
1 tablespoon finely grated fresh ginger
2 garlic cloves, crushed
2 tablespoons grated palm sugar
    (jaggery) or brown sugar
juice of 1 lime
1 green mango
a handful coriander (cilantro) leaves
1 long red chilli, seeded and thinly sliced
2 tablespoons vegetable oil

Preheat the oven to 180°C (350°F/Gas 4). Put the piece of pork belly in a large saucepan and cover with cold water. Bring to the boil, then remove the pork and rinse it in fresh water. Pat dry with paper towel.

In a large roasting tin, combine the soy sauce, rice wine, chicken stock, ½ teaspoon of the Chinese five-spice, the short red chilli halves, cinnamon stick, star anise, ginger and garlic. Add the pork to the roasting tin, skin side up, and rub the skin with the remaining Chinese five-spice. Add enough water to ensure that most of the pork is covered by liquid but the skin is dry. Cover the roasting tin with foil and bake for 4 hours.

Remove the cooked pork from the tin and put it on a large tray. Cover and refrigerate overnight. Reserve 375 ml (13 fl oz/1½ cups) of the cooking liquid.

Cut the pork belly into eight strips. Put the reserved cooking liquid in a saucepan with the palm sugar and lime juice and bring to the boil. Reduce the heat and allow to simmer for 10 minutes.

Finely julienne or grate the green mango into a bowl and add the coriander and sliced chilli. Toss to combine. Meanwhile, heat the oil in a large non-stick frying pan and fry the pieces of pork belly until they are crisp and browned.

Put two pieces of pork belly onto each serving plate, spoon some of the sauce over them, then top with the mango salad.

sugar spiced pork cutlets

....

SERVES 4

2 tablespoons brown sugar
½ teaspoon Chinese five-spice
4 pork cutlets
1 teaspoon sesame oil
1 garlic clove, finely chopped
1 tablespoon finely grated fresh ginger
2 tablespoons oyster sauce
2 tablespoons Chinese rice wine
1 tablespoon light soy sauce
1 tablespoon lemon juice
1 tablespoon olive oil
steamed Chinese greens, to serve

Preheat the oven to 180°C (350°F/Gas 4). Combine the brown sugar and
Chinese five-spice in a bowl, then add the pork cutlets. Rub the sugar mixture
all over the cutlets and set them aside.

Heat a small saucepan over medium heat and add the sesame oil, garlic and
ginger. Stir for 1 minute, then add the oyster sauce, rice wine and soy sauce.
Simmer for 1–2 minutes, then add the lemon juice and pour into a serving jug.

Heat a large non-stick frying pan over medium heat. Add the olive oil and
sear the cutlets for 1 minute on each side, then put them onto a baking tray and
cook in the oven for 10 minutes, or until cooked.

Serve the cutlets with steamed Chinese greens and a drizzle of the sauce.

Lots of lovely Asian flavours are worked into this lean pork cutlet, so serve with plenty of steamed greens to soak up the soy ginger sauce.

roast chicken leg quarters with figs and almonds

....

SERVES 4

4 chicken leg quarters
4 figs, halved
80 g (2¾ oz/½ cup) blanched almonds
4 garlic cloves, crushed
juice of 2 lemons
2 tablespoons honey
green salad, to serve

Preheat the oven to 180°C (350°F/Gas 4). Put the chicken, figs, almonds and garlic into a roasting tin. Pour over the lemon juice, then drizzle with the honey. Season with sea salt, then cover the roasting tin with foil. Bake for 40 minutes, then remove the foil and bake for a further 20 minutes.

Serve with a green salad.

Roasted chicken leg quarters are a great way to feed a group with ease. In this recipe, the chicken, figs and almonds are all roasted together. When the chicken is done, simply serve with a large bowl of green salad.

barramundi fillets with ginger butter

SERVES 4

4 tablespoons butter, softened
½ onion, finely diced
1 tablespoon finely grated fresh ginger
2 tablespoons finely chopped coriander (cilantro) leaves
4 x 185 g (6½ oz) barramundi fillets
1 tablespoon vegetable oil
steamed broccolini, to serve

Put half of the butter in a frying pan over low–medium heat and add the onion and ginger. Sauté until the onion is soft and golden brown. Remove from the heat and set aside to cool. When the onion mixture has cooled, fold in the remaining butter and the coriander.

Rinse the barramundi fillets in cold water and pat them dry with paper towel. Heat the oil in a frying pan over high heat and add the barramundi fillets skin side down. Fry for 3–5 minutes until the skin is lightly browned, then flip the fish over and cook the other side for a further 3–5 minutes, depending on the thickness of the fillets.

Serve with steamed broccolini and a dollop of ginger butter.

creamed rice with pomegranate molasses

SERVES 6

1 tablespoon pomegranate molasses
   (see Note on page 126)
2 tablespoons light brown sugar
110 g (3¾ oz/½ cup) short-grain white rice
1 vanilla bean
500 ml (17 fl oz/2 cups) milk
4 tablespoons caster (superfine) sugar
125 ml (4 fl oz/½ cup) thin (pouring/whipping)
   cream, whipped
fresh pomegranate seeds, mango slices
   or strawberries, to serve

Put the molasses, brown sugar and 1 tablespoon boiling water in a small bowl and stir until the sugar has dissolved. Set aside.

Rinse the rice in cold water, then drain. Rub the vanilla bean between your fingertips to soften it, then split it along its length. Using the tip of a knife, scrape most of the seeds into a saucepan. Add the vanilla bean, milk and sugar to the pan and bring it almost to the boil. Add the rice, reduce the heat to low and simmer gently for 30 minutes, stirring occasionally.

When the rice has cooked, remove the pan from the heat and lift out the vanilla bean. Transfer the rice to a bowl and allow to cool completely.

When the mixture has cooled, fold through the whipped cream. Divide the creamed rice among six bowls, then drizzle with some of the pomegranate molasses syrup and serve with fresh pomegranate seeds, mango slices or strawberries.

I love pomegranate molasses, though I normally use it with vegetables and salads. However, I made this creamed rice one day and wanted something a little tart to go with it. The molasses just seemed like a good idea at the time, and still does.

This is a beautiful crumble. You can make it as six small crumbles or in one large dish. The topping is flavoured with brown sugar and coconut while the base is fresh plums with a dash of rosewater. Crumbles should be cooked until the juices are bubbling over the sides of the dish. A sure sign that the fruit is deep in conversation with the sweet crumble.

As a result of this photograph, I have given this recipe the nickname of 'the drowning figs tart' ... all those poor figs awash in a sea of crisp sugary batter. Just think, you'll be doing them a favour if you take a slice and gobble them up.

rosy plum crumbles

SERVES 6

10 blood plums (about 800 g/1 lb 12 oz in total)
75 g (2½ oz/⅓ cup) caster (superfine) sugar
1 teaspoon rosewater
110 g (3¾ oz/½ cup, firmly packed) dark brown sugar
60 g (2¼ oz/½ cup) plain (all-purpose) flour
45 g (1½ oz/½ cup) desiccated coconut
75 g (2½ oz) unsalted butter
whipped cream or thick (double/heavy)
      cream, to serve

Preheat the oven to 180°C (350°F/Gas 4). Slice the plums, removing the stones, and put them in a bowl. Add the caster sugar and rosewater and toss until the plums are well coated in sugar. Set aside for 10 minutes.

Toss the brown sugar, flour and coconut together in a bowl. Rub the butter in with your fingertips until the mixture resembles breadcrumbs. Set aside.

Stir the plums again to ensure they are well coated, then divide among six 150 ml (5 fl oz) ovenproof bowls, piling the plums above the top of the bowls as they will cook down quite a bit.

Top the plums with the coconut mixture, then sit the bowls on a baking tray and bake for 30 minutes, or until the crumbles are golden and the juices are bubbling over the sides of the bowls. Serve warm with cream.

fig and burnt butter tart

SERVES 8

6 figs, quartered
22 cm (8½ inch) pre-baked shortcrust tart case
      (see page 183 for recipe)
3 eggs
165 g (5¾ oz/¾ cup) caster (superfine) sugar
3 tablespoons plain (all-purpose) flour
185 g (6½ oz) unsalted butter

Preheat the oven to 180°C (350°F/Gas 4). Arrange the figs in the tart case with the narrow ends pointing up.

Beat the eggs and sugar until they are pale and fluffy then fold in the flour. Heat the butter in a saucepan over high heat, and when it begins to froth and turn a biscuit colour pour the hot butter into the egg mixture and continue to beat for 1 minute. Pour the filling over the figs and bake for 25 minutes or until the filling is cooked and golden brown. Allow the tart to cool before serving.

chocolate plum cake

165 g (5¾ oz/¾ cup, firmly packed) dark brown sugar
280 g (10 oz/2¼ cups) plain (all-purpose) flour
185 g (6½ oz) cold unsalted butter
2 teaspoons baking powder
3 tablespoons dark cocoa powder
¼ teaspoon salt
230 g (8 oz) caster (superfine) sugar
3 eggs, lightly whisked
185 ml (6 fl oz/¾ cup) milk
16 small plums (about 550 g/1 lb 4 oz),
    halved and stones removed
ice cream or thick (double/heavy) cream,
    to serve

Preheat the oven to 180°C (350°F/Gas 4). Grease a 25 cm (10 inch) spring-form cake tin. Put the brown sugar into a bowl with 30 g (1 oz/¼ cup) of the flour and mix together. Add 3 tablespoons of the cold butter (leave the rest at room temperature to soften) and rub the butter in with your fingertips until the mixture resembles coarse breadcrumbs.

Sift the remaining flour into a mixing bowl along with the baking powder, cocoa powder and salt. Put the caster sugar and softened butter in a separate bowl and cream together using electric beaters, then add the eggs and mix well. Add half of the flour mixture, then half of the milk, mixing well after each addition. Mix in the remaining flour mixture, then the remaining milk.

Pour the batter into the prepared cake tin and arrange the plum halves on top, cut side down. Sprinkle with the brown sugar mixture and bake for 50–60 minutes, or until a skewer inserted into the centre of the cake comes out clean. Allow the cake to cool before turning out of the tin.

This is a rich chocolate cake made extra moist with the addition of a sugary plummy topping that cooks a little bit soft and a little bit crisp. Serve with ice cream, double cream or whipped cream tinged with ground cinnamon.

This is a lovely light dessert with a big flavour punch. The nutty cigar of filo is flavoured with cardamom and cinnamon and served with a pomegranate reduction that has a lovely sour sweetness.

Dip the pastry into the reduction and enjoy the melding of flavours. You can eat them like this with a strong black coffee or turn them into more of a dessert with a dollop of cream.

fig and filo parcels with a pomegranate syrup

SERVES 6

80 g (2¾ oz/¾ cup) ground almonds
6 dried figs, finely chopped
2 tablespoons honey
2 teaspoons finely grated lemon zest
2 teaspoons lemon juice
1 teaspoon ground cinnamon
¼ teaspoon ground cardamom
3 sheets filo pastry
40 g (1½ oz) butter, melted
2 tablespoons icing (confectioners') sugar
250 ml (9 fl oz/1 cup) fresh pomegranate juice
110 g (3¾ oz/½ cup) caster (superfine) sugar
thick (double/heavy) cream and pomegranate seeds, to serve

Preheat the oven to 180°C (350°F/Gas 4). Line a baking tray with baking paper.

In a bowl, combine the ground almonds, figs, honey, lemon zest, lemon juice, cinnamon and cardamom.

Put one of the sheets of filo on a clean dry surface and brush with some of the melted butter. Cover with another sheet of filo and butter the surface again before repeating with the final sheet of filo. Cut the sheet of filo in half lengthways, then into thirds crossways (you should have six small rectangles). Spread the ground almond mixture over the rectangles, leaving 1 cm (½ inch) clear at the end of each rectangle. Roll them up to form six tight rolls. Brush any remaining butter over the rolls before placing them on the prepared baking tray. Bake for 5 minutes each side or until they are golden brown all over. Remove to a wire rack and dust with icing sugar.

Put the pomegranate juice and caster sugar into a small saucepan and bring to the boil. Continue to cook until the juice has reduced by half and has formed a syrup.

Serve the filo fingers with a dollop of cream, a drizzle of pomegranate syrup and a scatter of fresh pomegranate seeds.

maple panna cotta

SERVES 4

2 tablespoons maple syrup
250 ml (9 fl oz/1 cup) thin (pouring/whipping) cream
250 ml (9 fl oz/1 cup) milk
2 tablespoons sugar
1 vanilla bean
2 teaspoons powdered gelatine
4 ripe figs, halved

Spoon the maple syrup into four 150 ml (5 fl oz) ramekins, allowing
2 teaspoons per ramekin. Put them into the freezer.

Put the cream, milk and sugar into a small saucepan. Rub the vanilla bean
between your fingers to soften it. Using the tip of a sharp knife, split the vanilla
bean in half along its length and add it to the cream. Cook over low heat for
10 minutes, then remove from the heat and discard the vanilla bean. Sprinkle
the gelatine over the warm cream and stir for 2 minutes to ensure that it has
dissolved thoroughly into the mixture.

When the cream has cooled, remove the ramekins from the freezer. Gently
pour the cream over the maple syrup. Cover with plastic wrap, then refrigerate
for several hours.

Just before serving, run a sharp knife around the inside of the ramekins and
turn out onto serving plates. Serve with the fig halves.

One day I had a complete disaster with a crème caramel recipe. The details of which my ego won't allow me to go into. But it did make me think of an easy way to combine cream and caramel. What if you didn't have to make the caramel but simply used maple syrup, I thought, and what if you used vanilla panna cotta as a base? Here's the answer.

This is a great recipe to make for a large gathering. The baked pears can be cooked en masse and served simply with cream or ice cream. If you want to be especially naughty you could even drizzle them with melted dark chocolate.

maple baked pears

4 Corella pears, halved
2 teaspoons unsalted butter, softened
2 tablespoons maple syrup

Preheat the oven to 180°C (350°F/Gas 4).

Scoop out the core of the pears with a teaspoon. Place the pears skin side up on a chopping board and with a sharp knife take a thin slice from the top of each pear (this will give them a flat surface to sit on). Put the pears on a shallow baking tray skin side down. Rub the butter over the surface of the pears, then fill each of the hollowed cores with the maple syrup. Cover with foil and bake for 1 hour.

Serve with thick cream or vanilla ice cream.

pear and cardamom tart

SERVES 6–8 SLICES

180 g (6¼ oz/1¾ cup) almond
    meal
110 g (4¾ oz) unsalted butter
110 g (3¾ oz/½ cup) caster
    (superfine) sugar
3 eggs
½ teaspoon ground cardamom
3 teaspoons unsweetened cocoa
    powder
1 x 25 cm (10 inch) pre-baked
    shortcrust tart case
    (see page 183 for recipe)
2 ripe beurre bosc pears,
    quartered, cored and
    thickly sliced

Preheat the oven to 180°C (350°F/Gas 4). Put the almond meal, butter, all the sugar except for 2 tablespoons, the eggs, cardamom and cocoa powder into a food processor and blend to form a thick paste. Carefully spoon and spread the mixture into the pre-baked tart case.

Arrange the pear slices in a fan over the top of the almond layer. Bake for 20 minutes.

Take the tart out of the oven and sprinkle the top with the remaining sugar. Return the tart to the oven for a further 10 minutes and then test to check that the tart is cooked all the way through. Allow it to cool slightly before transferring to a serving plate.

ginger rhubarb

SERVES 4–6

250 g (9 oz) caster (superfine)
    sugar
1 star anise
4 cm (1½ inch) piece fresh ginger,
    peeled and cut into
    thick rounds
800 g (1 lb 12 oz/2 bunches)
    rhubarb, trimmed, rinsed
    and stalks cut into 10 cm
    (4 inch) lengths

Put the sugar in a large saucepan with 500 ml (17 fl oz/2 cups) water. Add the star anise and ginger. Bring to the boil over high heat, stirring until the sugar has dissolved. Reduce the heat to low to bring the syrup to a simmer.

Cook the rhubarb in batches in the simmering syrup for 2–4 minutes, or until it begins to soften. Remove the rhubarb with a pair of tongs and place into a deep serving dish. When all the rhubarb has been cooked, increase the heat and reduce the syrup by half. Pour the hot syrup over the rhubarb.

Serve warm with custard or chilled with ice cream.

This is one of my favourite images. It was from one of my first books and I love the fact it's brown and graphic. Two words not normally associated with each other. Anyway, there's something lovely about the combination of pear and cardamom and this tart is delicious served with a generous spoonful of ice cream.

A simple recipe for ginger-spiced rhubarb, which can be served with custard, ice cream or honey yoghurt, or can be used as the base for a fruit crumble. My rhubarb-growing grandfather used to spoon stewed rhubarb onto his morning toast, which I think is going a bit far.

These filo fingers are filled with a spiced pistachio paste and the fruit is dripping with a sweet cardamom and rosewater syrup. All in all, it's a rich evocation of the flavours and perfumed aromas of the Middle East.

spiced filo with fig and pomegranate salad

....

SERVES 4

70 g (2½ oz/½ cup) shelled pistachio nuts
2 tablespoons honey
2 teaspoons lemon zest
2 teaspoons lemon juice
1 teaspoon cinnamon
2 sheets of filo pastry
2 tablespoons butter, melted
4 figs, thinly sliced
2 pomegranates
thick (double/heavy) cream, to serve

cardamom syrup
110 g (3¾ oz/½ cup) caster (superfine) sugar
1 teaspoon lemon juice
5 cardamom pods, lightly crushed
½ teaspoon rosewater

Preheat the oven to 160°C (315°F/Gas 2–3). Line a baking tray with
baking paper.

To make the cardamom syrup, put the sugar, lemon juice and cardamom
pods in a small saucepan with 250 ml (9 fl oz/1 cup) water. Bring slowly to the
boil, stirring until the sugar has dissolved completely, then reduce the heat and
simmer for 5 minutes. Remove from the heat and stir in the rosewater. Allow to
cool and set aside.

Finely chop the pistachios in a food processor or blender and put them into
a bowl with the honey, lemon zest, lemon juice and cinnamon. Stir to combine.

Lay a sheet of filo pastry on a clean work surface and brush with melted
butter. Fold one-third of the sheet over, then fold the remaining third over the
top, to make a rectangle measuring about 15 x 28 cm (6 x 11¼ inches). Put the
pastry on the baking tray, brush with more butter and spread all the pistachio
mixture over the top. Repeat the folding and buttering process with the
remaining sheet of filo, then lay it over the pistachio mixture and firmly press
to form a sandwich. Brush the top with any remaining butter.

Using kitchen scissors, cut the finished pastry rectangle in half widthways.
Cut each of those pieces in half, then in half again. You should have eight pastry
strips, each measuring 3 x 15 cm (1¼ x 6 inches). Bake for 10 minutes, or until
golden brown, then cool on a wire rack.

Arrange the figs in the centre of four dessert plates. Remove the seeds
and juice from the pomegranates and spoon them over the figs. Dollop some
cream in the centre and cross two pastry strips over each plate. Drizzle with
the cardamom syrup.

WINTER

comfort food

There really is something lovely about hibernating through the
winter months even if it doesn't get seriously cold where you live.
Guilt free days curled up inside with occasional forays out into
the damp air, it's all about comfort—and the food we eat mirrors
this. I have to say I love writing recipes for this time of the year it's
all warm soups, slow cooked meats and rich desserts. Actually,
these are some of my favourite foods and a style of cooking,
which involves time but very little effort. It's the food of the great
indoors, where time is spent occasionally checking a simmering
pot or casserole dish. It's also the perfect time to have friends
around to enjoy a warming bowl of goodness.

espresso french toast with banana

SERVES 4

2 x 100 g (3½ oz) panettone
4 large egg yolks
125 ml (4 fl oz/½ cup) strong freshly
    brewed espresso coffee
2 tablespoons unsalted butter
2 bananas, sliced on the diagonal
80 ml (2½ fl oz/⅓ cup) maple syrup

Trim the top and bottom off each panettone, then cut each cake widthways into four round discs approximately 2 cm (³/4 inch) wide. Whisk the egg yolks and coffee together until well combined. Dip the panettone slices, one at a time, into the egg mixture, ensuring they are well coated.

Heat the butter in a non-stick frying pan over medium heat. When it starts to sizzle, add the panettone slices and fry for 1–2 minutes on each side, until crisp and golden.

Put the panettone on serving plates, pile with the banana slices and drizzle with the maple syrup.

Bananas and maple syrup are a great caramel-ly combination, especially when combined with espresso-flavoured French toast. This is the ultimate decadent breakfast.

Corn fritters are such a scrumptious breakfast, as they somehow combine freshness with a slight stodginess in the same mouthful. An impressive feat and exactly what you want on a cold morning. The mixture should be prepared close to the cooking time, so if you are planning a big breakfast for friends, make the batter and the chopped vegetables ahead of schedule but don't combine the two until the last minute.

corn fritters

SERVES 6

125 g (4½ oz/1 cup) plain (all-purpose) flour
1 teaspoon baking powder
1 teaspoon smoked paprika
1 tablespoon sugar
1 teaspoon sea salt
2 eggs
125 ml (4 fl oz/½ cup) milk
4 corn cobs
½ red capsicum (pepper), diced
4 spring onions (scallions), thinly sliced,
     plus extra, to serve
2 large handfuls coriander
     (cilantro) leaves, chopped
80 ml (2½ fl oz/⅓ cup) vegetable oil
crisp bacon or fried eggs, to serve

Sift the flour, baking powder and paprika into a large bowl. Stir in the sugar and sea salt, then make a well in the centre.

In a separate bowl, whisk together the eggs and milk. Gradually add the liquid ingredients to the dry, stirring to make a stiff, lump-free batter. Cover and refrigerate until ready to use.

Using a sharp knife, cut the corn kernels away from the cobs and put the kernels in a large bowl. Add the capsicum, spring onion and coriander. Toss to combine.

Just before serving, slowly work the batter into the fresh ingredients. Heat 2 tablespoons of the oil in a large non-stick frying pan over medium heat. Using 1 tablespoon at a time, drop spoonfuls of batter into the hot pan. Cook for a few minutes, or until golden underneath, then flip the fritters and cook for a further 2 minutes, or until quite crisp. Keep warm while you cook the rest of the fritters, adding more oil as necessary; you should end up with around 30 small fritters.

Scatter with the extra spring onion and serve with crisp bacon or fried eggs.

spiced carrot soup

SERVES 4 AS A STARTER OR LIGHT MEAL

2½ tablespoons butter
1 red onion, diced
1 teaspoon ground cumin, plus
    extra, to serve (optional)
3 tablespoons red lentils
500 g (1 lb 2 oz) carrots, peeled
    and finely chopped
1.5 litres (52 fl oz/6 cups)
    vegetable stock
thick (double/heavy) cream,
    to serve (optional)

Melt the butter in a saucepan over medium heat, then add the onion and cumin. Cook until the onion is soft and transparent, then add the lentils and carrot. Stir for 1 minute before pouring in the vegetable stock. Bring to the boil, then reduce the heat to low so the soup is at a slow simmer. Continue to cook for 40 minutes, or until the carrot is soft and beginning to fall apart.

Remove the pan from the heat and allow to cool slightly. Transfer the mixture to a blender, a few ladlefuls at a time, and blend to a smooth purée. Return to a clean saucepan and heat over low heat when ready to serve.

Season with sea salt and freshly ground black pepper. Serve with a sprinkling of ground cumin or a dollop of cream, if desired.

chilli bacon penne

SERVES 4 AS A STARTER OR LIGHT MEAL

400 g (14 oz) penne pasta
3 tablespoons butter
1 red onion, diced
2 garlic cloves, finely chopped
2 red chillies, seeded and
    finely chopped
3 bacon slices, chopped
4 roma (plum) tomatoes,
    coarsely chopped
70 g (2½ oz/½ cup) finely grated
    parmesan cheese, to serve
8 roughly torn basil leaves, to serve

Bring a large saucepan of salted water to the boil. Cook the penne until *al dente*, then drain and return it to the warm pan.

Meanwhile, melt the butter in a large frying pan over medium heat, add the red onion, garlic and chillies and sauté until the onion is soft and transparent. Add the bacon and cook for 2 minutes. Add the tomato, cover and allow to simmer over low heat for 10 minutes. Using a spoon, roughly break up the tomato, then season with sea salt and freshly ground black pepper.

Add the tomato sauce to the pan with the pasta and stir over low heat until it coats all the pasta. Divide among four warmed pasta bowls and sprinkle with parmesan cheese and basil leaves.

This is an old-fashioned style of soup that always reminds me of my grandmother. She made it with lamb and not bacon but it had the same vegetables and barley. I say her soup because she only ever made the same soup and it was served to us whenever we went to her place. It seems boring to us now but as children it was deeply comforting to eat the same soup out of the same bowls every time.

barley and bacon soup

SERVES 4 AS A STARTER OR LIGHT MEAL

2 tablespoons butter
2 garlic cloves
3 leeks, white part only, rinsed and finely chopped
1 teaspoon thyme leaves
½ teaspoon finely chopped rosemary leaves
4 bacon slices, finely diced
1 large carrot, grated
2 celery stalks, thinly sliced
175 g (6 oz) pearl barley
2 litres (70 fl oz/8 cups) chicken or vegetable stock
a handful flat-leaf (Italian) parsley leaves
50 g (1¾ oz/⅓ cup) grated parmesan cheese

Melt the butter in a large saucepan over medium heat. Cook the garlic and leek, stirring, for 1 minute. Add the thyme, rosemary and bacon. Continue to cook until the leek is soft and translucent. Add the carrot, celery and barley and cook for a further 5 minutes, stirring. Pour in the stock, cover with a lid and reduce the heat to a simmer. Cook for 1 hour, or until the barley is soft.

Ladle the hot soup into four bowls and top with the parsley and parmesan.

roast pumpkin and coconut soup

SERVES 4 AS A STARTER OR LIGHT MEAL

1 kg (2 lb 4 oz) jap or kent pumpkin (winter squash), peeled and cut into chunks
2 tablespoons olive oil
1 garlic clove, thinly sliced
2 leeks, white part only, rinsed and thinly sliced
1 red chilli, seeded and finely chopped
500 ml (17 fl oz/2 cups) vegetable stock
200 ml (7 fl oz) coconut milk
a handful coriander (cilantro) leaves

Preheat the oven to 180°C (350°F/Gas 4).

Put the pumpkin in a roasting tin and roast for 30 minutes, or until cooked through and golden brown.

Put the olive oil in a large saucepan with the garlic and leek and cook over medium heat until the leek is soft and translucent. Add the pumpkin, chilli and vegetable stock and simmer for 10 minutes. Remove from the heat and allow to cool slightly.

Transfer the soup mixture to a blender and purée until smooth. Return to a clean saucepan and stir in the coconut milk. Reheat over medium heat, then ladle into four bowls and scatter with coriander.

chestnut and mushroom soup

SERVES 4 AS A STARTER OR LIGHT MEAL

1½ tablespoons butter
1 onion, finely chopped
1 garlic clove, finely chopped
400 g (14 oz) Swiss brown mushrooms, coarsely chopped
300 g (10½ oz) tinned chestnuts, drained
1 litre (35 fl oz/4 cups) chicken stock
2 tablespoons crème fraîche or light sour cream
flat-leaf (Italian) parsley, to scatter

Heat the butter in a saucepan over medium heat and add the onion and garlic. Sauté for 5 minutes, or until the onion is soft and translucent. Add the mushrooms, cover and cook for 5 minutes, or until the mushrooms have reduced by half. Add the chestnuts and chicken stock and simmer for 15 minutes. Season to taste with sea salt and allow to cool.

Transfer the soup to a food processor or blender and purée in batches until smooth. Return to the saucepan and gently reheat. Ladle the soup into four warmed bowls and top with a dollop of crème fraîche and some freshly ground black pepper.

It may seem slightly more labour intensive, but roasting the pumpkins intensifies the flavours and ensures that they are all a little caramelised. The coconut milk adds an extra creaminess and the fresh coriander adds a lovely bite to this richly flavoured soup.

Chestnuts used to be an ingredient that always reminded me of Europe because of the smell of them roasting in the street. In Australia they were quite difficult to find, however we are now producing our own and you can get the whole range—fresh, tinned and frozen. I love using chestnuts in both savoury and sweet recipes. In this recipe I've teamed them with mushrooms, garlic and a dollop of crème fraîche.

Minestrone is by its very nature a hearty soup. Its history in Italy dates back to ancient times and it has always been a peasant-style soup based on seasonally available vegetables. It was only in later years with the introduction of tomatoes, potatoes and pasta to Italy that it became the soup we know today. As a peasant soup it had to fill hungry tummies and it still does.

minestrone

150 g (5½ oz/¾ cup) dried cannellini (white) beans
2 tablespoons butter
100 g (3½ oz) pancetta, finely chopped
2 red onions, finely chopped
2 carrots, peeled and grated
2 celery stalks, thinly sliced
3 large ripe tomatoes, coarsely chopped
1 litre (35 fl oz/4 cups) chicken or vegetable stock
1 dried bay leaf
1 rosemary sprig
2 zucchini (courgettes), diced
100 g (3½ oz) green beans, trimmed and cut into
    2 cm (¾ inch) lengths
60 g (2¼ oz) risoni
2 tablespoons tomato paste (concentrated purée)

Soak the dried beans overnight in plenty of water. Drain.

Heat the butter in a large saucepan over medium heat. Add the pancetta and the soaked beans and cook for 1 minute. Add the onion, carrot and celery and cook until the onion is soft and translucent. Add the tomato, stock, bay leaf, rosemary and 500 ml (17 fl oz/2 cups) water. Bring to the boil, then reduce the heat to a gentle simmer and cook for 40 minutes, or until the beans are cooked through.

Add the zucchini, green beans, risoni and tomato paste and cook for a further 30 minutes, stirring often, until the risoni is *al dente*. Remove the bay leaf and rosemary sprig. Season to taste with sea salt and freshly ground black pepper.

seared prawns with tomato parsley broth

SERVES 4 AS A STARTER OR LIGHT MEAL

16 raw large prawns (shrimp), peeled, deveined,
    tails left intact and shells and heads reserved
1 tablespoon butter
a pinch of saffron threads
1 teaspoon sea salt
6 black peppercorns
4 flat-leaf (Italian) parsley stalks, coarsely chopped and leaves reserved
2 spring onions (scallions), coarsley chopped
1 teaspoon fish sauce
2 tablespoons lemon juice
2 vine-ripened tomatoes, seeds removed and flesh diced
buttered crusty bread, to serve

Put the prawns in a bowl, cover and refrigerate until ready to use.

Melt the butter in a saucepan over medium heat. Add the saffron, cook
for 1 minute, then add the prawn shells and heads and cook for 2–3 minutes,
stirring occasionally, until all of the heads have turned orange. Add 1 litre
(35 fl oz/4 cups) water, the sea salt and peppercorns. Add the parsley stalks
and half of the spring onion and bring to the boil. Once boiling, reduce the heat
and simmer for 30 minutes.

Remove the stock from the heat and strain into a bowl. Rinse the saucepan,
then pour in the strained stock and continue to simmer over low heat. Add
the fish sauce, lemon juice and tomato. Roughly chop the reserved parsley
leaves and add to the broth with the remaining spring onion.

Heat a non-stick frying pan over high heat. When the pan is hot, sear
the prawns on both sides until they turn pink and begin to curl up.

Ladle the stock into four warmed pasta bowls and pile the prawns in
the centre. Serve with buttered crusty bread.

In case you hadn't noticed, I use a lot of parsley. It's probably my favourite herb. I think it's because parsley brings a lovely freshness to food and it is fresh flavours that really excite me. But I think it's also because I grew up with a kitchen garden that had runaway parsley and mint, two herbs that were thrown into everything in an attempt to control their growth!

A nice warming winter stew that isn't too heavy. I always think it should be eaten while wearing a home-knitted Aran-style sweater having just come in from a walk along a rainswept coastline. My imagination does run away with me sometimes!
The stew could be spooned over creamy mashed potato or simply served with warm crusty bread.

fish stew

....

SERVES 4-6

3 tablespoons olive oil
500 g (1 lb 2 oz) snapper fillets, cut into 5 cm (2 inch) pieces
500 g (1 lb 2 oz) ling fillets, cut into 5 cm (2 inch) pieces
a pinch of saffron threads
2 spring onions (scallions), thinly sliced
250 ml (9 fl oz/1 cup) dry white wine
1 litre (35 fl oz/4 cups) fish stock
2 celery stalks, thinly sliced
400 g (14 oz) tin chopped tomatoes
100 g (3½ oz/½ cup) long-grain white rice
1 teaspoon dried oregano
1 dried bay leaf
a handful flat-leaf (Italian) parsley, roughly chopped
juice of 1 lemon
mashed potato, to serve (optional)

Heat the oil in a large heavy-based saucepan over medium heat. Working in batches, add the fish pieces and lightly cook them on all sides, removing the fish as it becomes opaque. Set aside. Add the saffron and spring onion to the hot saucepan, stir once or twice in the warm oil, then stir in the wine. Allow to simmer for 1 minute, then add the fish stock, celery, tomatoes, rice, oregano and bay leaf. Bring to the boil, then reduce the heat and simmer for 20 minutes, or until the rice is cooked.

Just before serving, remove the bay leaf, return the fish to the pan and add the parsley. Stir in the lemon juice and season to taste with sea salt and freshly ground black pepper. Serve on its own, or with creamy mashed potato, if desired.

thai-style meatballs in a tomato, ginger and tamarind sauce

SERVES 4

2 long red chillies, seeded and coarsely chopped

4 garlic cloves, crushed

grated zest of 1 lime

1½ tablespoons fish sauce

2 tablespoons finely grated fresh ginger

6 spring onions (scallions), thinly sliced, plus extra to garnish

6 cm (2½ inch) lemongrass stem, white part only, coarsely chopped

a handful mint, coarsely chopped

700 g (1 lb 9 oz) minced (ground) pork

125 ml (4 fl oz/½ cup) vegetable oil

1 onion, finely chopped

400 g (14 oz) tin tomatoes, coarsely chopped

2 tablespoons tamarind purée (see Note on page 79)

1 tablespoon caster (superfine) sugar

noodles, cooked, to serve

Put the chilli, garlic, lime zest, fish sauce, half of the ginger, the spring onion, lemongrass and mint in a food processor and process until the mixture is very finely chopped. Add the minced pork and process, using the pulse action, until combined. Transfer to a bowl and season well with sea salt and freshly ground black pepper.

Form the mixture into walnut-sized balls. Heat 80 ml (2½ fl oz/⅓ cup) of the oil in a large frying pan over medium heat. Cook the meatballs for 4–5 minutes each side until golden; you may need to do this in batches. Drain on paper towel.

Put the onion and the remaining ginger in a large saucepan or flameproof casserole dish with the remaining oil and cook over medium heat until the onion is soft and translucent. Add the tomatoes, tamarind purée, caster sugar and 100 ml (3½ fl oz) water. Simmer for 2–3 minutes, then add the meatballs. Continue to simmer for 20 minutes.

Serve the meatballs with noodles and garnish with the extra spring onion.

One complaint I often get about my books is that the food looks so beautiful! I thought that this was the perfect picture with which to discuss the art of food styling. This is a delicious Asian twist on the more traditional Italian-style meatballs and spaghetti. I'll say right now, that I don't expect anyone at home to beautifully arrange their noodles. I know the food tastes delicious and will do so no matter how it's plonked into the bowl at home. However as a food stylist, my job is to make the meals look enticing. In the studio I can spend forever trying to find the perfect piece of basil but I certainly don't do that in my own kitchen!

This is definitely a curl-up-on-a-Sunday-night kind of dinner. Barley and lamb is a classic old-fashioned combination that still works beautifully, however I've brought it into this century with a scatter of fresh flat-leaf parsley and finely grated parmesan.

barley with lamb and vegetables

SERVES 4

2 tablespoons olive oil
2 garlic cloves, crushed
500 g (1 lb 2 oz) boneless lamb shoulder,
    cut into 2 cm (¾ inch) cubes
1 leek, white part only, rinsed and thinly sliced
1 carrot, peeled and diced
2 celery stalks, thinly sliced
1 dried bay leaf
200 g (7 oz/1 cup) pearl barley
1 litre (35 fl oz/4 cups) vegetable stock
2 tablespoons finely grated parmesan cheese
2 tablespoons finely chopped flat-leaf (Italian) parsley

Heat the olive oil in a large saucepan over high heat and cook the garlic and lamb until the lamb is lightly browned all over. Add the leek, carrot, celery and bay leaf and cook for 2–3 minutes, or until the leek is beginning to soften. Add the barley and cook for a further 2–3 minutes, stirring occasionally. Add the vegetable stock and season to taste with sea salt and freshly ground black pepper. When the stock is beginning to boil, cover and reduce the heat to low. Cook for 30 minutes, or until most of the stock has been absorbed by the barley.

Spoon into four bowls and top with the parmesan and parsley.

cinnamon lamb meatballs

SERVES 4

500 g (1 lb 2 oz) minced
    (ground) lamb
2 garlic cloves, crushed
2 tablespoons finely chopped
    flat-leaf (Italian) parsley
finely grated zest of 1 lemon
120 g (4¼ oz) pine nuts,
    coarsely chopped
1 egg
60 ml (2 fl oz/¼ cup) olive oil
1 leek, white part only, rinsed
    and thinly sliced
400 g (14 oz) tin tomatoes
½ teaspoon ground cinnamon
1 tablespoon lemon juice
risoni or couscous, to serve
green salad, to serve

Put the lamb mince, garlic, parsley, lemon zest, pine nuts
and egg into a bowl and combine well. Season with sea
salt and freshly ground black pepper. Roll the mixture into
walnut-sized balls.

Heat a frying pan over high heat and add 1 tablespoon of
the olive oil. Cook the meatballs in two batches until they are
browned all over (3–4 minutes each batch), then remove them
to a plate.

Put a small flameproof casserole dish or large saucepan
over medium heat and add the remaining olive oil and the leek.
Sauté until the leek is soft, then add the tomatoes, cinnamon
and lemon juice. Add the meatballs and simmer for a further
20 minutes.

Serve with risoni or couscous and a leafy green salad.

sausage and bean stew

SERVES 4

2 x 400 g (12 oz) tinned cannellini
    (white) beans, rinsed
5 ripe roma (plum) tomatoes,
    coarsely chopped
400 g (14 oz) tin chopped
    tomatoes
2 leeks, white part only, rinsed
    and coarsely chopped
8 garlic cloves, peeled
1 tablespoon thyme leaves
250 ml (9 fl oz/1 cup) white wine
350 g (12 oz) good-quality spicy
    thick sausages
15 g (½ fl oz/½ cup) coarsely
    chopped flat-leaf (Italian)
    parsley
crusty bread, to serve

Preheat the oven to 180°C (350°F/Gas 4).

Put the beans, tomato, leek, garlic, thyme and white wine
into a casserole or ovenproof dish.

Prick the sausages with a fork and then sear them in a frying
pan over high heat, until they are browned on all sides. Cut the
sausages into bite-sized pieces and put them into the casserole
dish. Lightly stir everything together, then cover the dish with
a lid or foil and cook in the oven for 1 hour.

Sprinkle with the parsley and serve with warm crusty bread.

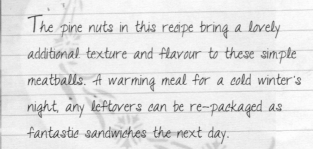

The pine nuts in this recipe bring a lovely additional texture and flavour to these simple meatballs. A warming meal for a cold winter's night, any leftovers can be re-packaged as fantastic sandwiches the next day.

A few of the mums at school have thanked me for this one. It's a great make-ahead meal that can be reheated after a long afternoon wrangling children into various after-school activities. It's warm and hearty and will quickly fill hungry children.

Such an elegant meal, this is a must for those who love the flavour of lemon. The fried sage is not only beautiful to look at but it adds a light crunch and delicate flavour to the soft and creamy risotto.

lemon risotto with fried sage

SERVES 4

1 litre (35 fl oz/4 cups) chicken stock
2 tablespoons butter
a pinch of saffron threads
2 garlic cloves, crushed
2 leeks, white part only, rinsed and thinly sliced
finely grated zest of 1 lemon
330 g (11½ oz/1½ cups) arborio rice
125 ml (4 fl oz/½ cup) white wine
juice of 1 lemon
70 g (2½ oz/½ cup) finely grated parmesan cheese
80 ml (2½ fl oz/⅓ cup) olive oil
16 large sage leaves

Put the chicken stock in a saucepan and bring to the boil. Reduce the heat to a low simmer.

Heat the butter in a large saucepan over medium heat. Add the saffron, garlic and leek and cook until the leek is soft and translucent. Add the lemon zest and rice and stir for 1 minute, until the grains are well coated and glossy. Add the white wine and simmer, stirring, until the liquid is absorbed. Add 250 ml (9 fl oz/1 cup) of the stock and simmer, stirring, until it is absorbed. Repeat with another cup of stock, and when the liquid has been absorbed add the lemon juice and another cup of stock.

Cook for 20 minutes or until all the liquid has been absorbed and test the rice to see if it is *al dente*. If it is still slightly undercooked, add the remaining stock and simmer until the stock has reduced and the rice is coated in a creamy sauce.

Fold the parmesan through the risotto and spoon into four warm bowls.

Heat the olive oil in a small frying pan and fry the sage leaves for 1 minute. Drain and cool on paper towel, then arrange the sage leaves on top of the risotto and season with freshly ground black pepper.

rice with tomatoes and spinach

....

SERVES 6 AS A SIDE DISH OR LIGHT MEAL

1 tablespoon butter

500 g (1 lb 2 oz/1 large bunch) English spinach,
    washed, drained and finely chopped

400 g (14 oz/2 cups) basmati rice

3 tablespoons light olive oil

½ teaspoon ground turmeric

1 teaspoon ground cumin

1 red onion, thinly sliced

2 vine-ripened tomatoes, finely chopped

750 ml (26 fl oz/3 cups) vegetable stock

Melt the butter in a frying pan over medium heat. Add the spinach, then
cover and cook until dark green and softly wilted. Set aside.

Wash the rice several times until the water runs clear.

In a large saucepan, heat the olive oil over medium heat and sauté the
turmeric, cumin and onion for 5–7 minutes, or until the onion is golden
and slightly caramelised. Add the rice and cook, stirring, for 1 minute.

Squeeze any excess moisture from the spinach and add it to the rice
with the tomato and stock. Stir once, then bring to the boil. Cover, turn the
heat down to the lowest setting, and cook for 25 minutes.

It's the basmati rice that gives this dish its special flavour, though it is also lightly spiced with cumin and turmeric, too. It's a wonderfully warming and nutritious meal that can be eaten by itself as well as making a great side dish for a large gathering.

Apart from vegetarians, who doesn't love a lamb shank? They really are the most glorious winter food; soft and dissolving meat, with rich pan juices. I've lightened the flavour of these shanks with a fresh tomato and parsley salsa, which gives them a bit of zing. If you're a real shank fan, you could serve this recipe any time of the year.

lamb shanks with fresh tomato and parsley salsa

....

SERVES 4

1 tablespoon olive oil
8 small or 4 large lamb shanks, French trimmed
1 onion, coarsely chopped
2 garlic cloves, finely chopped
250 ml (9 fl oz/1 cup) vegetable stock
125 ml (4 fl oz/½ cup) red wine
2 tablespoons tomato paste (concentrated purée)
2 small rosemary sprigs
1 dried bay leaf
6 anchovy fillets, coarsely chopped
4 tomatoes, diced
a handful flat-leaf (Italian) parsley
    leaves, coarsely chopped
1 tablespoon grated lemon zest

Preheat the oven to 180°C (350°F/Gas 4).

Heat the olive oil in a lidded large flameproof casserole dish. Cook the shanks in batches until they are golden brown, then transfer them to a plate. Put the onion and garlic in the casserole dish and cook, stirring, until the onion is translucent. Add the vegetable stock, wine, tomato paste, rosemary, bay leaf and anchovies. Return the lamb shanks to the casserole, cover with the lid, and cook them in the oven for 2 hours.

Combine the tomato, parsley and lemon zest in a bowl.

Divide the lamb shanks among four warm pasta bowls. Spoon some of the sauce over the shanks, then top with the tomato salsa.

beef and potatoes

SERVES 4

2 tablespoons vegetable oil
300 g (10½ oz) fillet steak, thinly sliced
2 onions, thinly sliced
1 teaspoon finely grated fresh ginger
1 large carrot, peeled and cut into chunks
500 g (1 lb 2 oz) waxy potatoes, peeled and
    cut into bite-sized chunks
3 tablespoons soy sauce
55 g (2 oz/¼ cup) brown sugar
2 tablespoons mirin
steamed greens, to serve

Heat the oil in a flameproof casserole dish. Sauté the beef for 2–3 minutes, until the meat is brown on both sides; you might need to do this in batches so that the meat does not stew.

Remove the beef to a clean plate and add the onion and ginger to the casserole dish. Sauté for 2–3 minutes or until the onion is soft. Add the carrot, potato, meat, soy sauce, sugar, mirin and 400 ml (14 fl oz) water. Bring to a simmer and skim away any froth that rises to the surface.

Simmer over low heat for 30 minutes, or until the potatoes are cooked through. Spoon over a bed of steamed greens and serve immediately.

I called this dish 'beef and potatoes' as a bit of a joke because although it's terrifically simple to make, the flavours are quite complex. It's actually beef and potatoes Kyoto style, but if I called it that people might shy away from trying something different. So beef and potatoes it is. For a more hearty meal, spoon it over brown rice and serve steamed greens on the side.

Cumin and coriander seeds taste so much nicer if they are roasted and then ground. It's the toasty flavours that form the basis of this dish, however, if you don't have a grinder or are a little pushed for time, you can use ground cumin and coriander. This paste is a simple but effective way to introduce a lot of flavour to fish fillets.

The chipotle chilli is an ingredient that is often used in Mexican cooking and is actually the smoked and dried jalapeño chilli. It can sometimes be found in its dried form but is most commonly found as chipotles en adobo in tins. This is a version where the dried chilli is cooked in a rich tomato sauce. It's a great smoky hot flavour to add to lentils and sauces and in this recipe it gives the lentils a bit of a kick.

spice-crusted fish

SERVES 4

2 tablespoons coriander seeds

2 tablespoons cumin seeds

1½ tablespoons sea salt

1 garlic clove

2 large handfuls flat-leaf (Italian) parsley leaves

2 tablespoons extra virgin olive oil

4 x 200 g (7 oz) blue eye cod or white fish fillets

2 tablespoons light olive oil

mashed potato, to serve

lemon wedges, to serve

Preheat the oven to 180°C (350°F/Gas 4).

Put the coriander and cumin seeds on a baking tray and roast them in the oven for 2 minutes, or until they begin to darken. Remove, cool briefly and put them in a mortar or spice grinder with the salt and a generous amount of black pepper. Grind to a powder, then add the garlic, parsley and extra virgin olive oil, working the mixture to a thick paste.

Rinse the fish in cold water and pat dry with paper towel.

Pat the paste onto the top of each of the fish fillets, forming a thickish crust that completely covers the surface.

Heat the light olive oil in a large ovenproof frying pan over high heat until it begins to shimmer. Add the fish to the pan, crust-side down. Sear for 1 minute, turn it over and cook for another minute. Put the pan in the oven for 5 minutes. Serve the fish on a bed of mashed potato with lemon wedges on the side.

spiced lentils with lamb cutlets

SERVES 4

2 tablespoons olive oil

2 garlic cloves, crushed

1 red onion, finely diced

1 teaspoon finely chopped tinned chipotle chilli

1 teaspoon ground turmeric

105 g (3½ oz/½ cup) puy or tiny blue-green lentils

400 g (14 oz) tin chopped tomatoes

12 small lamb cutlets, French-trimmed

a handful coriander (cilantro) leaves

Put the olive oil in a saucepan over medium heat. Add the garlic, onion, chilli and turmeric and sauté for 5 minutes, or until the onion is soft and translucent. Add the lentils and cook for 1 minute, stirring well. Stir in the tomatoes and 500 ml (17 fl oz/ 2 cups) water, then cover and simmer for 40 minutes, or until the lentils are tender. Season to taste with sea salt and freshly ground black pepper. Keep warm.

Heat a large non-stick frying pan over high heat. Add the lamb cutlets and sear until the surface looks slightly bloody. Turn the cutlets over and cook for 1–2 minutes. Transfer to a warm plate, cover loosely with foil and rest for a few minutes.

Spoon the lentils onto four warmed serving plates. Top with the cutlets and scatter over the coriander.

lamb curry

SERVES 4

1 kg (2 lb 4 oz) lamb shoulder, trimmed and cut into cubes
3 tablespoons olive oil
juice of 2 lemons
1 tablespoon finely grated fresh ginger
2 teaspoons garam masala
2 onions, thinly sliced
400 g (14 oz) tin chopped tomatoes
2 tablespoons tomato paste (concentrated purée)
3 green chillies, seeded and cut into strips
250 ml (9 fl oz/1 cup) beef stock
10 mint leaves, finely chopped
300 g (10½ oz) plain yoghurt
steamed white rice, to serve

Put the lamb into a large ceramic dish and add 2 tablespoons of the olive oil, the lemon juice, ginger and garam masala. Massage the ingredients into the lamb to ensure it is well coated. Cover with plastic wrap and allow to marinate for 3 hours in the refrigerator.

Heat the remaining oil in a large heavy-based saucepan and add the onion. Cook for a few minutes until the onion is soft, then add the lamb—depending on the size of your pan you may need to cook the lamb in batches. Cook for several minutes until browned. Add the tomatoes, tomato paste, chilli and stock and return the rest of the lamb to the pan if necessary. Allow to simmer, stirring occasionally, over low heat for 1½ hours, or until the liquid has reduced and the lamb is coated in a rich, thick sauce.

Meanwhile, stir the mint leaves into the yoghurt. Serve the lamb spooned over steamed rice with a dollop of minty yoghurt.

pepper steaks with creamy mash

SERVES 4

40 g (1½ oz) butter
2 garlic cloves, crushed
10 French shallots, halved
1 tablespoon green peppercorns
300 ml (10½ fl oz) veal stock
1 tablespoon olive oil
4 x 200 g (7 oz) fillet steaks
creamy mashed potato, to serve

Heat the butter in a small saucepan. As it starts to froth, add the garlic, shallots and green peppercorns. Sauté over low heat for 10 minutes, or until the shallots are soft and turning lightly golden. Add the stock and keep at a low simmer.

Heat a non-stick frying pan over high heat. Rub the olive oil over the beef fillets and sear for 3 minutes, or until the surface looks slightly bloody. Turn the steaks over, reduce the heat and cook for a further 4–5 minutes. Transfer to a warm plate, cover loosely with foil and allow to rest for a few minutes.

Serve the steaks on a bed of creamy mashed potato and spoon the warm peppercorn sauce over the top and season with sea salt.

Lamb shoulder is the perfect cut for this rather old-school style curry. The shoulder falls apart during the long cooking time and becomes soft and succulent. The tomatoes add a lovely richness and the minty yoghurt pulls the whole thing together.

A great steak with a creamy mash is one of those perfect meals, however both the potatoes and meat are heavy flavours and they need a bit of punch. Green peppercorns are preserved in vinegar so they bring a bit of heat and bite to this dish, which is also enhanced by the silky smooth texture of the shallots.

This bistro classic really needs no introduction. It might be the blokey option on the menu but I'm normally the one that orders it as you can tell a lot about a restaurant by how well they do the simple standards.

A couple of years ago, dried baby figs appeared on the scene and I had lots of fun playing around with various ways to use them. This is a lovely tagine, flavoured with ginger and saffron, and featuring these tiny figs. They are sweet so you do need to add the lemon juice at the end to pull back some of that sweetness.

red wine steaks

SERVES 4

250 ml (9 fl oz/1 cup) red wine
2 garlic cloves, finely chopped
½ teaspoon finely chopped
    rosemary
125 ml (4 fl oz/½ cup) olive oil
4 x 185 g (6½ oz) sirloin steaks
2 tomatoes
2 Lebanese (short) cucumbers
1 teaspoon balsamic vinegar
2 tablespoons extra virgin olive oil
1 teaspoon sumac

Put the wine, garlic, rosemary and olive oil in a large non-metallic bowl and mix together well.

Add the steaks to the marinade. Turn them to ensure all the meat is thoroughly coated, then cover and marinate in the refrigerator for 2–3 hours.

Remove the steaks from the marinade and season well with freshly ground black pepper. Sear on a hot barbecue or in a frying pan over high heat for 2–3 minutes on each side. Turn the heat down and cook for a further 2 minutes or until the steak are cooked to your liking. Remove from the heat and cover with foil. Allow to rest for a few minutes.

Cut the tomatoes and cucumbers into chunks and put them in a serving bowl. Add the vinegar, extra virgin olive oil and sumac. Toss to combine and season lightly with sea salt.

Serve the steaks on four plates with chips and the tomato and cucumber salad.

chicken and baby fig tagine

SERVES 4

3 tablespoons extra virgin olive oil
2 onions, diced
2 garlic cloves, crushed
2 teaspoons finely grated
    fresh ginger
10 saffron threads
1 teaspoon freshly ground
    black pepper
1 kg (2 lb 4 oz) skinless chicken
    thigh fillets, coarsely chopped
500 ml (17 fl oz/2 cups) chicken
    stock
120 g (4¼ oz) dried baby figs
100 g (3½ oz) dates
2 dried bay leaves
1 cinnamon stick
20 g (¾ oz/⅔ cup) chopped flat-
    leaf (Italian) parsley leaves
2 tablespoons lemon juice
couscous, to serve

Heat the extra virgin olive oil in a large saucepan over medium heat and cook the onion, garlic, ginger, saffron and black pepper, stirring, for 2–3 minutes, or until the onion is soft and golden brown.

Add the chicken and cook until it is lightly golden all over. Add the chicken stock, figs, dates, bay leaves and cinnamon stick. Bring to the boil, then reduce the heat and cook gently for 30 minutes.

Season to taste with sea salt and freshly ground black pepper. Add the parsley and lemon juice. Serve with couscous.

vanilla panna cotta with toffee apples

....

SERVES 8

875 ml (30 fl oz/3½ cups) thin
    (pouring/whipping) cream
finely grated zest and juice of
    2 lemons
110 g (3¾ oz/½ cup) caster
    (superfine) sugar
2 vanilla beans, halved lengthways
3 gelatine sheets

toffee apples

4 green apples, peeled, cored
    and cut into eighths
3 tablespoons caster
    (superfine) sugar
1 teaspoon cinnamon

Whip 250 ml (9 fl oz/1 cup) of the cream and put it in the fridge.

Put the remaining cream, lemon zest and juice, sugar and vanilla beans in a saucepan and heat gently over low heat to melt the sugar; do not let it boil.

Take the pan off the heat and, using a sharp knife, scrape the seeds from the inside of each of the vanilla beans into the cream mixture, keeping the pods for later use.

Soak the gelatine sheets in a bowl of cold water. When the sheets are soft, squeeze out any excess water and stir them into the warm cream mixture. Set aside to cool.

Fold the chilled whipped cream through the cooled cream mixture, then pour the combined mixture into eight tea cups or dariole moulds, cover with plastic wrap and chill in the fridge for 3 hours or overnight.

To make the toffee apples, toss the apple pieces in the sugar, cinnamon and 2 tablespoons water. Then tip them into a heavy-based frying pan over medium heat and let them caramelise and brown. Turn each of the apple pieces as they begin to caramelise and remove them from the pan when they are cooked on both sides.

Serve the panna cotta in their cups with the apples on the side, or turn them out by dipping the base of each mould briefly into a bowl of hot water and upending them onto the plate. Give them a little shake to loosen them. Serve with the warm toffee apples.

bread and butter pudding

....

SERVES 4–6

butter, for greasing
1 x 450 g (1 lb) loaf of brioche
1 teaspoon ground cinnamon
3 eggs
3 tablespoons caster (superfine)
    sugar
500 ml (17 fl oz/2 cups) cream
4 tablespoons golden syrup

Preheat the oven to 180°C (350°F/Gas 4). Lightly butter a ceramic baking dish.

Remove the crusts from the brioche loaf, slice the loaf, then cut into triangles. Arrange the triangles over the base of the baking dish and sprinkle with the cinnamon. Put the eggs, sugar and cream into a bowl and whisk together. Pour the cream mixture over the brioche and drizzle the golden syrup over the pudding.

Bake for 25 minutes, or until the pudding is set and is a nice golden brown colour.

This is a lovely zesty lemony panna cotta with a side serve of slightly caramelised apple slices that have a lovely toffee apple flavour.

Bread and butter pudding is an old-school favourite. I used brioche because it brings an extra richness to this simple dessert. This pudding is drizzled with golden syrup, however you can also flavour the brioche with marmalade, strawberry jam or quince paste.

Not many people cook quinces, which is a shame. Although they do take a bit of patience, the rewards are great. They taste like a perfumed pear but their firm flesh make them perfect for poaching and slow cooking. This recipe takes three or four hours but don't worry, most of that time is spent with the quinces simmering in a pot – filling the house with the most wonderful aromas. The simmering slowly turns the white-fleshed quinces to a beautiful ruby rose.

This is a light and creamy version of the traditional creamed rice. The rice is slowly cooked in milk and then allowed to cool before being folded through whipped cream. It's a little indulgent but perfect to serve with stewed fruit or some simple berries.

slow-poached quinces

....

SERVES 4

110 g (3¾ oz/½ cup) sugar
2 tablespoons honey
2 dried bay leaves
1 star anise
2 large quinces, peeled, cut into 8 segments and cored
thick (double/heavy) cream or vanilla ice cream, to serve

Put the sugar, honey, bay leaves and star anise into a saucepan and cover with
500 ml (17 fl oz/2 cups) water. Stir until the sugar has dissolved. Add the quince
segments and cook over medium heat until the syrup has come to a slow simmer.
Reduce the heat to low, cover with a lid and continue to cook the quinces for
3½ hours, removing the bay leaves after the first hour.

When cooked, the quince segments should be soft and the syrup and
quinces a wonderful rose colour. Serve the quinces with a drizzle of syrup
and cream or ice cream.

vanilla creamed rice

....

SERVES 4

110 g (3· oz/½ cup) short-grain white rice
650 ml (22½ fl oz) milk
1 vanilla bean, split and seeds removed
4 strips lemon zest
2 tablespoons sugar
125 ml (4 fl oz/½ cup) thin (pouring/whipping)
    cream, whipped
fruit to serve

Rinse the rice in cold water and drain it.

Put the rice, milk, vanilla bean and seeds, lemon zest and sugar in a
saucepan and stir over medium heat until the sugar has dissolved. Bring to the
boil, then reduce the heat to low and simmer gently for 20–25 minutes, stirring
occasionally.

When the rice has cooked, allow it to cool to room temperature, remove the
vanilla bean and lemon zest, then fold in the whipped cream. Spoon into four
small bowls and top with seasonal fruit.

hazelnut affogato

375 ml (13 fl oz/1½ cups) milk
250 ml (9 fl oz/1 cup) thin (pouring/whipping) cream
2 tablespoons finely ground toasted hazelnuts
4 egg yolks
125 g (4½ oz) caster (superfine) sugar
4 teaspoons hazelnut or coffee liqueur
4 shots of freshly brewed espresso coffee

To make the ice cream, pour the milk and cream into a heavy-based saucepan and add the ground hazelnuts. Place the saucepan over medium heat and bring the mixture just to simmering point. Remove from the heat.

In a large bowl, whisk the egg yolks with the sugar until light and creamy. Whisk in a little of the warm milk mixture, then add the remaining liquid and whisk to combine.

Rinse and dry the saucepan, then pour the mixture back into the pan. Cook over medium heat, stirring constantly with a wooden spoon, until the mixture thickens and coats the back of the spoon. Quickly remove from the heat, strain into a chilled bowl and allow to cool completely.

Churn in an ice-cream machine according to the manufacturer's instructions, then spoon into a container and freeze for at least 1 hour before serving. If you don't have an ice-cream machine, pour the mixture into a metal bowl, cover with plastic wrap and freeze. Every hour, stir the ice cream with a fork, scraping the frozen bits from the side of the bowl and folding them back through the ice cream. Repeat until the ice cream is quite stiff, then freeze overnight.

To serve, scoop two small balls of ice cream into four small heatproof glasses or cups and pour a teaspoon of liqueur over each. Serve the espresso coffee on the side for guests to pour over their ice cream.

This recipe started life in one of my favourite cafés. I'd called in with a friend one hot afternoon and asked for two iced coffees. However supplies were low and they offered espresso poured over hazelnut gelato instead. Not a bad option and I instantly loved the coffee and hazelnut combination.

This has become such a classic but I still love the flavours. The more varied the dried fruit the better and nowadays, with all the dried berries and baby figs available, you can make quite an exciting combination. This fruit salad can be made for dessert but then re-used through the week with yoghurt for breakfast.

I didn't want to do another recipe for sticky date pudding ... but there is something lovely about baking and dates. So I let my mind wander to exotic market places and thought of cardamon and chocolate.

marinated fruit salad

SERVES 6

70 g (2½ oz) dried figs

70 g (2½ oz) dried apricots

70 g (2½ oz) pitted prunes

2 heaped tablespoons dried
cranberries

55 g (2 oz/¼ cup) sugar

3 tablespoons fresh orange juice

1 cinnamon stick

2 star anise

½ teaspoon orange flower water

300 g (10½ oz) natural yoghurt,
to serve

45 g (1½ oz/½ cup) toasted flaked
almonds, to serve

70 g (2½ oz/½ cup) toasted
pistachio kernels, to serve

Put the figs and apricots in a bowl with the prunes and
cranberries.

Put the sugar, orange juice, cinnamon stick and star anise in
a saucepan with 250 ml (9 fl oz/1 cup) water. Bring to the boil
over medium heat, stirring until the sugar has dissolved. Boil
gently for 5–6 minutes, until a light syrup forms. Remove from
the heat and add the orange flower water.

Pour the liquid over the prepared dried fruit and allow to
soak for several hours, or preferably overnight.

Serve accompanied by the yoghurt and sprinkled with the
toasted nuts.

chocolate, cardamom and date puddings

SERVES 4

185 g (6½ oz) pitted dates

125 g (4½ oz) butter, cubed

100 g (3½ oz) good-quality
dark chocolate

2 eggs

185 g (6½ oz/1 cup) dark
brown sugar

150 g (5½ oz) self-raising flour

1 teaspoon ground cardamom

2 tablespoons crushed
pistachios, to serve

thick (double/heavy) cream,
to serve

4 extra squares of chocolate
(optional)

Preheat the oven to 180°C (350°F/Gas 4). Grease four small
(250 ml/9 fl oz/1 cup) soufflé dishes with butter.

Put the dates in a saucepan with 250 ml (9 fl oz/1 cup) of
water and soften over a gentle heat. Mash the dates with a fork,
then add the butter and chocolate. Continue to cook until the
chocolate and butter have melted, then remove from the heat.

In a bowl, beat the eggs with the brown sugar until thick and
pale, then add the chocolate mix. Whisk to combine, then stir
the flour and ground cardamom through.

Pour the mixture into the soufflé dishes and place the dishes
in a baking tin. Pour water into the baking tin, making sure it
comes halfway up the sides of the soufflé dishes. Cover the tin
with a sheet of buttered foil. Bake for 35–40 minutes.

Remove the baking tin from the oven and carefully lift
out the soufflé dishes. Serve the puddings warm with crushed
pistachios and cream. For an extra chocolate hit, press a square
of chocolate into the centre of each hot pudding before serving.

vanilla-poached apricots

SERVES 6

200 g (7 oz/1¼ cups) dried
    apricots
1 vanilla bean, split
½ teaspoon rosewater
1 tablespoon honey
45 g (1½ oz/⅓ cup) toasted
    slivered almonds
260 g (9¼ oz/1 cup) plain
    yoghurt or custard

Put the apricots in a saucepan with the vanilla bean and
625 ml (2½ fl oz/2½ cups) water. Bring to the boil, then cover
and allow the fruit to simmer over low heat for 1 hour.

Remove the vanilla bean and stir in the rosewater and the
honey. Serve with the toasted almonds and yoghurt or a swirl of
warm custard.

rhubarb fool

SERVES 6

500 g (1 lb 2 oz/about 30 stalks)
    rhubarb, trimmed and cut into
    5 cm (2 inch) lengths
110 g (3¾ oz/½ cup) caster
    (superfine) sugar
juice of 1 orange
½ teaspoon ground cinnamon
300 ml (10½ fl oz) thin (pouring/
    whipping) cream, whipped
almond bread or pistachio biscotti,
    to serve

Put the rhubarb into a saucepan with the sugar, orange juice and
cinnamon. Cover and cook over low heat for 10 minutes, or until
the rhubarb has dissolved. Remove from the heat and set aside
for 1 hour to cool completely.

Gently fold the rhubarb through the whipped cream until
they are almost combined, yet still slightly distinct. Spoon into
dessert bowls and serve with almond bread or pistachio biscotti.

This is a delicious way to enjoy apricots all year round. The dried apricots are simmered with a vanilla bean until they are at the point of collapse. They can be served as a dessert with thick cream, ice cream or custard. Stewed like this they can also be combined with chopped apple as a surprising base for an autumn crumble.

I love stewed rhubarb. My grandfather always had a big clump of rhubarb growing in his garden and so I grew up with it spooned over ice cream or warm custard. In this recipe it's simply swirled through whipped cream.

WINTER

the hot oven

Food at this time of the year is all about the oven as its
warmth becomes the hub of the home, filling the house
with the delicious aromas of sweetly roasted meats and
vegetables. Winter is all about rich flavours that are a bit
sticky and caramelised, golden hues that transport us back
to childhood favourites which are the culinary equivalent
of a favourite blanket. I'm happy to be spending time in
the kitchen cooking meaty roasts, slow-cooked dinners and
desserts, baked cakes and tarts. All that food makes sense
in the cold and I'm more likely to keep an eye on a meal
that will spend several hours in the oven. In fact it's a good
excuse not to go out into the cold day.

You can make these in a big baking dish for a large group or individually in ramekins. This recipe serves two but it's an easy one to multiply into whatever amount you need. For a large group, spoon the cooked eggs and tomato mixture onto individual plates and serve the salsa and cheese in bowls for everyone to share.

pan-baked eggs with chilli salsa

SERVES 2

2 tablespoons olive oil
½ red onion, thinly sliced
½ red capsicum (pepper), coarsely diced
185 g (6½ oz/¾ cup) tinned chopped tomatoes
2 eggs
40 g (1½ oz) goat's cheese
buttered toast, to serve

chilli salsa
1 small Lebanese (short) cucumber, finely diced
1 red chilli, seeded and finely diced
a handful (6 g/½ cup) of coriander (cilantro) leaves

Preheat the oven to 180°C (350°F/Gas 4).

Put all of the chilli salsa ingredients in a bowl. Toss together and set aside.

Heat the olive oil in a small ovenproof frying pan. Add the onion and sauté over medium heat for 5 minutes, or until the onion is soft and translucent. Add the capsicum, tomatoes and 125 ml (4 fl oz/⅓ cup) water and cook for 5 minutes, or until the capsicum is beginning to soften. Season to taste with sea salt.

Make two small wells in the tomato mixture and break the eggs into them. Bake for 10 minutes, or until the whites of the eggs are cooked through.

Crumble the goat's cheese over the top and serve with the chilli salsa and buttered toast.

bacon and egg tart

SERVES 6

2½ tablespoons butter
3 onions, thinly sliced
6 bacon slices, thinly sliced
25 cm (10 inch) pre-baked
    shortcrust tart case
    (see page 206)
4 eggs
2 egg yolks
150 ml (5 fl oz) thin (pouring/
    whipping) cream
pinch of white pepper
herb salad, to serve

Preheat the oven to 180°C (350°F/Gas 4).

    Melt the butter in a saucepan over medium heat. Add the onion and cook for 10–15 minutes, or until lightly caramelised. Add the bacon and cook, stirring occasionally, for a further 10 minutes. Spread the bacon and onion over the base of the tart case.

    Whisk together the eggs, egg yolks and cream and season with sea salt and white pepper. Pour the mixture carefully into the tart case. Bake for 25 minutes, or until the top of the tart is golden brown. Serve with a herb salad.

potato and spinach frittata

SERVES 4

400 g (14 oz) waxy potatoes,
    peeled and cut into 4 cm
    (1½ inch) chunks
250 ml (9 fl oz/1 cup) vegetable
    stock
3 tablespoons olive oil
1 red onion, diced
2 celery stalks, thinly sliced
100 g (3½ oz/2¼ cups) baby
    English spinach leaves
6 eggs, lightly whisked
70 g (2½ oz/½ cup) finely
    grated parmesan cheese
green salad, to serve

Put the potato pieces in a deep frying pan and add the vegetable stock. Heat over high heat until most of the stock has evaporated. Reduce the heat to medium and add the olive oil, onion and celery, and season with sea salt and freshly ground black pepper. Toss so that all the vegetables are lightly coated in the oil. Cook for 2–3 minutes until the vegetables are slightly softened.

    Add the spinach leaves and cook over medium heat, stirring for 2–3 minutes, until the leaves have wilted. Pour the egg over the top, sprinkle with the parmesan and continue to cook for 10 minutes, or until the egg is almost set. Remove from the heat and place under a grill (broiler) until the cheese is golden and the frittata has begun to puff up. Serve warm with a green salad.

This tart is rich in bacon, egg and cream, so definitely a winter's breakfast or brunch. It can be served with a green salad or slow-roasted tomatoes.

Another great warm and filling weekend option, this frittata is heavy with potatoes, so serve it with a green salad or by itself with a spoonful of pesto or tapenade.

Baked ricotta is one of those wonderful dishes that is great to serve as part of a big antipasti selection. Which made me think about combining the whole antipasti plate in one easy-to-slice terrine. The spinach, olives and tomatoes give the creamy milkiness of the ricotta a real flavour boost.

layered ricotta bake

SERVES 4

1 bunch English spinach, trimmed and washed
1 kg (2 lb 4 oz/4⅓ cups) fresh ricotta cheese
15 pitted kalamata olives, finely chopped
8 basil leaves
80 g (2¾ oz) parmesan cheese, grated
8 semi-dried (sun-blushed) tomatoes, finely chopped
1 heaped tablespoon oregano leaves

Preheat the oven to 180°C (350°F/Gas 4).

Line a 12 x 22 cm (4½ x 8½ inch) terrine tin with baking paper.

Blanch the spinach leaves in boiling water, then drain and refresh under cold running water. Squeeze to remove any excess liquid and finely chop.

Put one-third of the ricotta in a small bowl. Add the chopped olives and stir to combine. Set aside.

Arrange the basil leaves in a line along the base of the terrine tin, then top with half the remaining ricotta. Sprinkle a tablespoon of the parmesan over the ricotta, then layer half the spinach over these cheeses. Top with half the tomatoes, all the oregano leaves and another tablespoon of parmesan. Cover this with all the olive-flavoured ricotta, sprinkle with another tablespoon of parmesan, then cover with the remaining spinach and tomato. Sprinkle with another tablespoon of parmesan then cover with the remaining ricotta. Sprinkle with the remaining parmesan.

Put the terrine tin on a baking tray and bake for 1 hour.

Remove from the oven and allow to cool in the tin, then turn out onto a serving plate. Serve with a green salad and crusty bread.

honey roast chicken with couscous salad

SERVES 4

1.8 kg (4 lb) whole organic chicken
20 g (1 bunch) rosemary
1 lemon, quartered
1 onion, quartered
3 tablespoons butter, softened
90 g (3¼ oz/¼ cup) honey
185 g (6½ oz/1 cup) instant couscous
1 tablespoon finely chopped lime pickle
a handful flat-leaf (Italian) parsley, coarsely chopped
a handful coriander (cilantro) leaves, coarsely chopped
2 tablespoons currants

Preheat the oven to 200°C (400°F/Gas 6).

Rinse the chicken and pat dry with paper towel. Scatter some of the rosemary sprigs into a roasting tin, then generously rub the chicken skin with sea salt and sit it on top of the rosemary, breast side up.

Put the lemon, onion and a few rosemary sprigs into the cavity of the chicken, then rub 2 tablespoons of the butter over the breast. Roast for 1 hour, then drizzle the honey over the chicken and roast for another 20 minutes. To check that the chicken is cooked, pull a leg away from the body, the juices that run out should be clear. Remove from the oven, cover loosely with foil and allow to rest for 10 minutes before carving.

Meanwhile, put the couscous in a bowl with the remaining butter and pour 250 ml (9 fl oz/1 cup) boiling water over the top. Cover and allow to sit for 5 minutes, then fluff up the grains with a fork. Cover again and leave for a further 5 minutes. Rub the grains with your fingertips to remove any lumps, then stir the lime pickle, parsley, coriander and currants through.

Carve the chicken and serve with the couscous and a spoonful of the roasting juices.

This is such a lovely meal and to be honest could be served at any time of the year. The honey makes the chicken skin something you'd happily die for and the couscous salad works nicely with the savoury-sweet meat. Make sure you spoon some of the sweet pan juices over the meat and couscous.

Dried wild mushrooms are a little bit expensive but they do go a long way and their flavour is wonderfully intense. Here they are combined with butter and served with a peppery roast beef. Well, that's Sunday lunch taken care of.

roast beef with wild mushroom butter

SERVES 4

2 tablespoons freshly ground black pepper
800 g (1 lb 12 oz) beef eye fillet, trimmed
10 g (¼ oz) dried porcini mushrooms
2½ tablespoons butter
1 tablespoon dijon mustard
mashed potato, to serve
steamed asparagus, to serve

Rub the pepper over the beef. Put the beef on a tray and leave it in the refrigerator, uncovered, overnight. Bring to room temperature before cooking.

Preheat the oven to 200°C (400°F/Gas 6). Put the mushrooms in a small bowl, cover with 125 ml (4 fl oz/½ cup) boiling water and soak for 10 minutes, or until soft. Drain, reserving the soaking liquid. Finely chop the mushrooms.

Heat 1 tablespoon of the butter in a small saucepan and add the mushrooms. Cook over medium heat for 5 minutes, then add the soaking liquid. Simmer for 10 minutes, or until most of the liquid has evaporated.

Coarsely chop the remaining butter and put it into a bowl. Add the mustard and warm mushrooms and mix well. Put the beef fillet into a roasting tin and roast for 10 minutes. Remove the fillet, turn it over and roast for a further 5 minutes.

Remove the meat from the oven, season with sea salt, cover with foil and allow to rest for 15 minutes.

Drain any juices from the roasting tin and add them to the mushroom butter. Stir to combine. Return the fillet to the oven for a further 15 minutes, for medium–rare, or 20 minutes for medium. Slice the beef thickly and serve topped with some of the mushroom butter, with creamy mashed potato and steamed asparagus on the side.

pork spare ribs

SERVES 4

250 ml (9 fl oz/1 cup) soy sauce
175 g (6 oz/½ cup) golden syrup or
    maple syrup
80 ml (2½ fl oz/⅓ cup) balsamic
    vinegar
4 tablespoons tomato paste
    (concentrated purée)
1 strip of orange zest
juice of 1 orange
1 tablespoon mustard powder
1 tablespoon finely grated
    fresh ginger
1 cinnamon stick
½ teaspoon ground cumin
½ teaspoon chilli powder
1 dried bay leaf
16–24 American-style pork ribs,
    no thicker than 2 cm (¾ inch)
polenta or mashed pumpkin,
    to serve

Put all of the ingredients except the ribs in a small saucepan. Mix well and bring to the boil, stirring to ensure that the marinade does not catch on the base of the pan. Remove the cinnamon stick and allow the marinade to cool a little.

Sit the ribs in a shallow dish and pour the marinade over them, ensuring all the ribs are well coated in the marinade. Cover and refrigerate for several hours, or preferably overnight.

Preheat the oven to 200°C (400°F/Gas 6). Line a ceramic baking dish with baking paper and arrange the ribs so they are lying flat. Pour any remaining marinade over the top.

Bake for 15 minutes, then turn the ribs over and bake for a further 15 minutes.

Serve on a bed of creamy polenta or mashed pumpkin, drizzled with the juices from the baking dish.

roast lamb with fresh mint aïoli

SERVES 6

20 g (1 bunch) rosemary
1.5 kg (3 lb 5 oz) leg of lamb
2 tablespoons olive oil
boiled waxy potatoes, to serve

aïoli
1 egg yolk
1 garlic clove, coarsely chopped
1 tablespoon white wine vinegar
125 ml (4 fl oz/½ cup) olive oil
30 mint leaves, finely chopped

Preheat the oven to 200°C (400°F/Gas 6). Scatter the rosemary sprigs over the base of a roasting tin, then sit the leg of lamb on top. Rub the surface of the lamb with a little of the olive oil, then rub sea salt and frshly ground black pepper into the skin. Place in the preheated oven. After 30 minutes remove the lamb and spoon some of the roasting juices over the meat. Return to the oven for a further 40 minutes. Transfer the lamb to a warmed serving plate and cover with foil. Allow the meat to rest for 15 minutes before carving.

While the lamb is resting, make the aïoli. Put the egg yolk in a small food processor with the garlic and vinegar. Blend, then pour the mixture into a large bowl. Slowly whisk in the oil until you have a thick mayonnaise. Stir in the mint leaves and enough warm water to make the aïoli the consistency of a thin sauce.

Carve the lamb and serve with the fresh mint aïoli and boiled potatoes.

Sticky, sweet and playful, pork spare ribs need little fanfare. These are richly flavoured with spices, ginger and orange. Ideally they should be marinated overnight and enjoyed with lots of finger-licking fun.

Lamb loves garlic and mint so it made sense to combine the two in a minty aïoli. Hopefully you'll have a little bit of both left over, as the two will make a fantastic sandwich combo. Just add watercress or thickly sliced tomato.

This is a lovely rich pork roast. The apples are cooked in the spicy pork marinade, turning them into a wonderful relish. Ask your butcher to remove the skin and score and slice it for you as few people have knives at home that are sharp enough to do this with ease.

cider-glazed pork loin

SERVES 6

500 ml (17 fl oz/2 cups) apple cider
3 tablespoons honey
3 garlic cloves, peeled and finely chopped
3 star anise
1 cinnamon stick
1 large red chilli, halved lengthways
2 dried bay leaves
1 kg (2 lb 4 oz) pork loin, skin cut off and reserved
3 green apples, peeled, cored and thickly sliced
1 tablespoon balsamic vinegar

Put the cider, honey, garlic, star anise, cinnamon, chilli and bay leaves in a bowl. Cut deep slashes diagonally over the pork loin and add the pork to the marinade. Roll it around so it is well coated, then cover it and put it in the fridge to marinate overnight.

Preheat the oven to 200°C (400°F/Gas 6). Transfer the pork to a roasting tin, cover with foil and roast for 40 minutes. To make the crackling, score the pork skin lightly with a very sharp knife and cut it into several strips. Put the strips in a roasting tin, brush them with water, sprinkle with salt and roast for 20 minutes or until the skin is golden brown and crackly. Drain off any fat.

While the meat is cooking, put the apples in a saucepan with 125 ml (4 fl oz/⅓ cup) of the marinating liquid. Bring to the boil and then leave to simmer for 15 minutes or until the liquid has reduced. Add the balsamic vinegar and season.

Uncover the pork and baste it with the pan juices. Cook it for a further 20 minutes or until the juices run clear when you insert a skewer into the meat. Stand the pork for 10 minutes before carving. Serve with the apple relish and crackling.

orecchiette with duck, orange and currants

SERVES 4

4 duck breasts, skin on
1 onion, diced
2 garlic cloves, chopped
1 leek, white part only, rinsed and
    thinly sliced
finely grated zest and juice of
    1 orange
1 carrot, peeled and chopped
1 celery stalk, thinly sliced
1 teaspoon thyme
250 ml (9 fl oz/1 cup) red wine
500 ml (17 fl oz/2 cups) chicken
    stock
2 tablespoons currants
400 g (14 oz) orecchiette
a handful flat-leaf (Italian) parsley

Cut the duck breasts into 2 cm (3/4 inch) wide slices.

Heat a heavy-based saucepan over medium heat and add the duck pieces in two batches. Cook until the meat is golden, then remove the meat and drain away most of the oil, leaving approximately 1 tablespoon in the base of the saucepan. Add the onion, garlic and leek and cook for 2–3 minutes. Add the orange zest, carrot and celery and cook for a further 10 minutes, stirring frequently. Add the thyme, wine, chicken stock, orange juice, currants and duck pieces. Simmer, partially covered, over low heat for 50 minutes or until the duck is falling apart. Season to taste with sea salt and freshly ground black pepper.

Cook the pasta until it is *al dente*, then drain and divide among four pasta bowls. Spoon the duck over the pasta and garnish with the parsley.

veal cutlets

SERVES 4

6 anchovy fillets
2 egg yolks
juice of 1 lemon
3 tablespoons olive oil
185 g (6½ oz) tin tuna, drained
1 tablespoon small salted capers,
    rinsed, drained and chopped
4 veal cutlets, French-trimmed
500 g (1 lb 2 oz/1 bunch) English
    spinach, rinsed and trimmed
flat-leaf (Italian) parsley leaves,
    to serve
lemon wedges, to serve

Preheat the oven to 180°C (350°F/Gas 4).

Put the anchovies, egg yolks, lemon juice, olive oil and tuna in a food processor or blender and purée to a thick sauce. Season with sea salt and freshly ground black pepper and stir in the capers.

Heat a large non-stick frying pan over high heat. Add the veal cutlets and sear for 2 minutes, then turn and sear for 1 minute. Place the cutlets on a baking tray and bake for 8–10 minutes. Remove from the oven, then cover loosely with foil and allow to rest for 5 minutes.

Meanwhile, put the spinach in the warm frying pan, then cover and cook over medium heat for 2 minutes, or until the spinach has turned emerald green.

Serve the cutlets scattered with parsley, accompanied by the spinach, lemon wedges and anchovy mayonnaise on the side.

Years ago when I was doing lots of catering, I used to make a lovely rich duck, orange and currant filling for little pastry turnovers. It was a flavour combination that came back to me years later when I was working on one of my books. This time around, it's become a lovely aromatic sauce for pasta.

This dish is for the carnivores in your life. Veal cutlets are almost a bit 'Flintstone' in their size and they are definitely not for the lapsed meat eater. However, I love their soft meaty flavour, which in this recipe is teamed with a tuna and anchovy sauce.

This is a richly flavoured shank recipe with potatoes, carrots and a sauce of veal and sherry. It's definitely a mid-winter special, however it is given a bit of zing with the gremolata, which is made of freshly grated horseradish, lemon zest and finely chopped parsley.

lamb shank and vegetable casserole

SERVES 4

85 g (3 oz/⅔ cup) plain (all-purpose) flour
4 lamb shanks (about 1.25 kg/2 lb 12 oz in total)
160 ml (5¼ fl oz) olive oil
2 leeks, white part only, rinsed and sliced into rounds
2 garlic cloves, crushed
1 teaspoon rosemary
250 ml (9 fl oz/1 cup) dry sherry
400 g (14 oz) tin chopped tomatoes
2 carrots, peeled and sliced
500 ml (17 fl oz/2 cups) veal stock
4 desiree or other all-purpose potatoes,
    peeled and cut into chunks

gremolata
3 tablespoons finely chopped flat-leaf (Italian) parsley
1 tablespoon finely grated lemon zest
1 tablespoon finely grated fresh horseradish

Preheat the oven to 200°C (400°F/Gas 6).

Put the flour into a plastic bag, add the lamb shanks and toss until well coated. Heat half of the olive oil in a large heavy-based frying pan and add the lamb shanks. Cook, in batches if necessary, until the shanks are browned on all sides. Transfer to a casserole dish and wipe the frying pan clean with paper towel.

Add the remaining oil to the frying pan and sauté the leek, garlic and rosemary for 4 minutes, or until the leek is starting to soften. Add the sherry and cook for a few minutes before adding the tomato and carrot. Stir for 1 minute, then pour the sauce over the shanks. Add the veal stock and season with sea salt and freshly ground black pepper. Cover and bake for 1 hour.

To make the gremolata, put all the ingredients onto a chopping board and, using a large knife, work the ingredients together as you chop.

Remove the casserole dish from the oven and turn the shanks around in the sauce. Add the potato, then cover and bake for a further 1 hour, or until the meat is tender and falling off the bone. Serve sprinkled with a little gremolata.

chicken and vegetable pot roast

SERVES 4–6

1.5 kg (3 lb 5 oz) whole organic
    chicken
1½ tablespoons butter, softened
4 slices of prosciutto
2 onions, cut into eighths
2 large carrots, cut into chunks
1 celery stalk, cut into 2 cm
    (¾ inch) lengths
1 turnip, peeled and cut into chunks
2 leeks, white part only, rinsed
    and sliced into 2 cm (¾ inch)
    rounds
3 all-purpose potatoes, peeled
    and cut into chunks
1 rosemary sprig
250 ml (9 fl oz/1 cup) dry
    white wine
250 ml (9 fl oz/1 cup) chicken stock
a handful flat-leaf (Italian) parsley,
    coarsely chopped

Preheat the oven to 180°C (350°F/Gas 4). Sit the chicken in a 3 litre (105 fl oz/12 cup) casserole dish. Rub the butter over the breast of the chicken, then cover with the prosciutto slices. Arrange the vegetables and rosemary around the chicken, then pour the wine and chicken stock over. Season well with sea salt and freshly ground black pepper. Cover and bake for 1 hour.

Remove the casserole dish from the oven and gently move the vegetables around. Using a large spoon, pour some of the juices over the chicken. Leave the lid off and roast for a further 30 minutes, or until the chicken is golden brown.

Place the chicken on a warm serving platter and arrange the vegetables around. Scatter over the parsley and drizzle with the sauces from the casserole dish.

roast new potatoes with lemon and rosemary

SERVES 6

1 kg (2 lb 4 oz) washed
    new potatoes
60 ml (2 fl oz/¼ cup) olive oil
juice of 1 lemon
6 rosemary sprigs

Preheat the oven to 180°C (350°F/Gas 4).

Put the potatoes in a large pan of cold water and bring to the boil. When the water is boiling, cover the pan with a lid and remove from the heat. Allow to sit for 15 minutes, then drain.

Put the boiled potatoes on a baking tray and, with the back of a large spoon, lightly crush each potato until it just begins to split. Drizzle the potatoes with the olive oil and lemon juice, then add the rosemary and a generous sprinkle of sea salt. Bake in the oven for 40 minutes, or until crisp and golden-brown.

A great meal for a wintry Sunday night, especially as any leftovers can be turned into a soup. The prosciutto brings a lovely rich warmth to the chicken flavours and also helps to ensure the breast meat doesn't dry out too much.

One of my desert island foods would have to be potatoes, and roast potatoes have to be at the top of the list. Roast potatoes come in many variations but infusing them with lemony rosemary gives them a really special flavour.

I know this seems like a strange way to cook beef but you'll have to trust me on this one. It does take a little bit of pre-planning and I find it helps to stick a Post-it note of times on the wall next to the oven. However, once you get the hang of it you can work the times into the meal preparation and it all comes together easily and always results in a perfect piece of beef.

peppered beef with pumpkin mash

SERVES 6

1.5 kg (3 lb 5 oz) beef eye fillet
2 tablespoons freshly ground black pepper
1 kg (2 lb 4 oz) pumpkin
150 g (5½ oz) butter
2 garlic cloves, crushed
25 g (1 oz/1 bunch) chives, finely chopped

Trim the fillet then rub the pepper into the surface. Put it on a tray and leave it in the fridge, uncovered, overnight.

Preheat the oven to 200°C (400°F/Gas 6). Put the fillet in a roasting tin and roast for 10 minutes before turning the meat and cooking for a further 5 minutes. Remove from the oven and season the fillet with sea salt. Cover with foil and rest for 15 minutes. Drain any juices from the pan and retain them to pour over the meat later.

Meanwhile, peel the pumpkin and cut into small pieces. Put it into a large saucepan with salted cold water and bring to the boil. Cook until tender. Melt the butter in a small saucepan over medium heat. Add the garlic and chives then simmer for a few minutes. When the pumpkin is cooked, drain and mash. Stir in the butter mixture and whip to a fluffy mash. Cover and set aside in a warm place.

Return the fillet to the oven for a further 15 minutes, for medium-rare, or 20 minutes for medium. Serve in thick slices with a drizzle of pan juices and a large spoonful of mashed pumpkin.

cinnamon swirls

MAKES 15

3 tablespoons milk, plus a little extra for glazing
7 g (1 sachet) dried yeast
250 g (9 oz/2 cups) plain (all-purpose) flour
2 tablespoons sugar
2 large eggs, whisked
100 g (3½ oz) butter, melted
1 teaspoon sea salt
165 g (5¾ oz/¾ cup) caster (superfine) sugar
3 teaspoons ground cinnamon
2 tablespoons poppy seeds (optional)

Preheat the oven to 180°C (350°F/Gas 4).

Heat the milk in a small saucepan until it is lukewarm. Remove from the heat and pour into a bowl, then sprinkle the yeast and 30 g (1 oz/¼ cup) of the flour over the milk. Stir to combine, then cover and allow to sit for 10 minutes or until the mixture looks as if it is beginning to bubble.

Add the remaining flour, sugar, egg, butter and sea salt. Stir to combine, then turn out onto a lightly floured surface. Knead the dough until it is smooth and elastic, then put it into a lightly oiled bowl. Cover and allow to sit in a warm place for 1 hour, or until the dough has doubled in size.

Punch the dough down and put it on a large piece of baking paper. Roughly flatten the dough, lightly flour its surface, then roll it with a rolling pin until the dough is approximately 30 x 45 cm (12 x 17¾ inches). Combine the caster sugar and the cinnamon and sprinkle over the dough. Roll the dough up widthways to form a long Swiss roll. Cut into 2 cm (¾ inch) slices and put the slices on a baking tray lined with baking paper. Cover with a clean tea (dish) towel and allow to rise for 30 minutes.

Brush the sliced dough with a little milk and, if you like, sprinkle with poppyseeds.
Bake in the oven for 15–20 minutes. Serve warm.

These buns are delicious straight from the oven, warm and spicy with that lovely poppy seed crunch. Serve them for breakfast or as a lovely warming afternoon tea.

There's something so wrong that it's right about this recipe. I was having a discussion with someone about how much I really loved muffins that were dense with bran. They replied that they liked the healthiness of bran but weren't too fussed with the flavour. So I suddenly thought that the earthy flavour of bran would work well with cocoa — one thing led to another and I had chocolate bran muffins with cranberry butter.

chocolate bran muffins with cranberry butter

MAKES 12

260 g (9½ oz/1 cup) plain yoghurt
100 ml (3½ fl oz) vegetable oil
2 eggs
2 teaspoons natural vanilla extract
335 g (11¾ oz/2⅔ cups) plain (all-purpose) flour
1 tablespoon baking powder
2 tablespoons dark unsweetended cocoa powder
35 g (1¼ oz/¼ cup) oat bran
½ teaspoon ground cinnamon
185 g (6½ oz/1 cup, lightly packed) light brown sugar
2 green apples, grated

cranberry butter
105 g (3½ oz/⅔ cup) dried cranberries
100 g (3½ oz) butter, softened

Preheat the oven to 180°C (350°F/Gas 4). Grease twelve holes in a standard muffin tin or line with paper cases.

Put the yoghurt, vegetable oil, eggs and vanilla in a bowl and whisk to combine. Sift the flour, baking powder and cocoa powder into a large bowl and add the oat bran, cinnamon, sugar and grated apple. Stir well so that the apple is well incorporated into the dry ingredients.

Pour the liquid ingredients over the dry ingredients and stir until they have just come together. Do not overmix.

Spoon the mixture into the prepared muffin holes. Bake for 30 minutes or until the tops feel firm and a skewer inserted into the centre comes out clean.

Meanwhile, to make the cranberry butter, put the cranberries and softened butter into a food processor and blend until the cranberries have worked their way into the butter. Spoon the flavoured butter onto a piece of baking paper and roll up to form a log. Refrigerate.

Serve the muffins warm with the cranberry butter.

date and banana loaf

160 g (5¾ oz/1 cup) chopped
    dates
2 bananas, mashed
2 tablespoons unsalted butter
½ teaspoon bicarbonate of soda
    (baking soda)
165 g (5¾ oz/¾ cup) caster
    (superfine) sugar
1 egg
250 g (9 oz/2 cups) self-raising
    flour, sifted
1 teaspoon baking powder
butter, to serve

Preheat the oven to 180°C (350°F/Gas 4). Grease and line a
10 x 20 cm (4 x 8 inch) loaf (bar) tin with baking paper.

Put the dates, banana, butter, bicarbonate of soda and sugar
in a bowl. Pour in 250 ml (9 fl oz/1 cup) boiling water, stir until
the sugar has dissolved, then leave to soak for a few minutes. Stir
the egg through, then fold the flour and baking powder through.

Pour the batter into the prepared tin and bake for 45 minutes,
or until a skewer inserted into the centre of the loaf comes out
clean. Cut into thick slices and serve toasted with butter.

treacle squares

SERVES 6

350 g (12 oz/1 cup) golden syrup
    or treacle
100 g (3½ oz/1 heaped cup)
    desiccated coconut
grated zest and juice of 1 lemon
¼ teaspoon ground cardamom
1 egg
6 sheets of filo pastry
3 tablespoons butter, melted
icing (confectioners') sugar,
    to serve
vanilla ice cream, to serve

Preheat the oven to 180°C (350°F/Gas 4). Line a 20 x 30 cm
(8 x 12 inch) baking tin with baking paper.

In a bowl, mix together the golden syrup, coconut, lemon
zest, lemon juice, cardamom and egg.

Remove the filo pastry from the packet and cover with a
slightly damp tea (dish) towel. Place a sheet of pastry on the
baking tray and brush with some of the melted butter. Repeat
with two more layers of pastry. Now spread the filling over
the pastry and top with another sheet of pastry. Brush with
melted butter, then repeat with the remaining two pastry sheets.
Generously brush the top sheet of pastry with butter, then bake
for 30 minutes, or until golden brown.

Turn the pastry out onto a clean chopping board. Cut into
large squares or triangles and dust generously with icing sugar.
Serve warm, with a scoop of vanilla ice cream.

Date loaves were once an important part of the afternoon tea repertoire. I fondly recall many afternoons as a child lurking near the table set for a long and chatty cup of tea, waiting for the date loaf to be cut and spread with butter.

This is a lovely light twist on a treacle tart — one of my favourite old-fashioned British desserts. I've taken the treacle tart filling and replaced the breadcrumbs with desiccated coconut, flavoured it all with cardamom and then layered it between sheets of filo pastry.

This is such a fun way to make an apple pie. The apple syrup will often set into a lovely thick richly apple-flavoured jelly which should be slathered all over the pie when it comes out of the oven.

rustic apple and blueberry pie

SERVES 6

> 3 green apples (500 g/1 lb 2 oz in total), peeled,
>   cored and cut into eighths
> 220 g (7¾ oz/1 cup) sugar, plus 3 tablespoons, extra
> grated zest and juice of 1 lemon
> 250 g (9 oz/2 cups) plain (all-purpose) flour
> 125 g (4½ oz) unsalted butter, cut into cubes and chilled
> 2–3 tablespoons chilled water
> 155 g (5½ oz/1 cup) blueberries
> whipped cream or custard, to serve

Put the apple in a saucepan with the sugar, lemon zest, 1 tablespoon of the lemon juice and 750 ml (26 fl oz/3 cups) water. Bring to the boil, then reduce the heat and simmer for 15–20 minutes, or until the apple is tender. Remove the apple with a slotted spoon, draining away as much liquid as possible, and allow to cool completely.

Meanwhile, continue simmering the syrup until it has reduced to one-third of its original volume. Remove the pan from the heat.

While the syrup is simmering, put the flour in a food processor with the butter and 1 tablespoon of the extra sugar. Process until the mixture begins to resemble breadcrumbs, then add the chilled water, starting with 2 tablespoons and adding more if needed. Process briefly until the dough comes together, then remove, cover with plastic wrap and chill in the refrigerator for 10 minutes.

Preheat the oven to 200°C (400°F/Gas 6). Roll the dough out between two large pieces of baking paper into a large circle about 30 cm (12 inches) in diameter, and about 5 mm (¼ inch) thick. Remove the top sheet of paper, then lift the lower sheet of baking paper and dough onto a baking tray.

Pile the cooled apple into the centre of the pastry, leaving a margin around the edge, then add the blueberries. Pull the dough up around the sides, scrunching it in over the fruit. Sprinkle with the remaining sugar, then bake for 40 minutes, or until the pastry is golden brown. Remove from the oven and allow to cool.

Brush some of the apple syrup over the pie before serving with whipped cream or custard.

chocolate crunch with fresh raspberries

MAKES 25 PIECES

250 g (9 oz) dark chocolate
50 g (1¾ oz) butter
3 tablespoons golden syrup
250 g (9 oz) digestive biscuits
    (cookies)
1 tablespoon unsweetened cocoa
    powder, plus extra, to dust
100 g (3½ oz) hazelnut meal
2 tablespoons brandy
fresh raspberries, to serve

Line a 15 cm (6 inch) square tin or container with baking paper.

Put the chocolate, butter and golden syrup in a small saucepan and melt over low heat.

In a large bowl, crush the digestive biscuits into small pieces, then add the cocoa and hazelnut meal. Pour the melted chocolate over the dry ingredients and stir to combine. Add the brandy and stir a few more times, before spooning into the tin. Top with another layer of baking paper and firmly press down to form a smooth top. Refrigerate for several hours.

Slice into small squares, dust with cocoa powder and serve with fresh raspberries.

winter fruit crumble

SERVES 6

400 g (14 oz/1 bunch) rhubarb,
    coarsely chopped
juice of 1 orange
6 dried figs, thinly sliced
2 green apples, peeled and
    coarsely chopped
55 g (2 oz/¼ cup) caster
    (superfine) sugar
60 g (2¼ oz/½ cup) plain
    (all-purpose) flour
100 g (3½ oz/½ cup, lightly
    packed) brown sugar
100 g (3½ oz/1 cup) almond meal
3 tablespoons unsalted butter
thin (pouring/whipping) cream
    or vanilla custard, to serve

Preheat the oven to 180°C (350°F/Gas 4). Toss the rhubarb with the orange juice, figs, apple and caster sugar and tip the mixture into an ovenproof dish.

Put the flour, brown sugar and almond meal in a bowl, and then add the butter and rub it into the dry ingredients until the mixture begins to resemble breadcrumbs.

Cover the fruit with this mixture and bake for 45 minutes. Serve with cream or vanilla custard.

This is a schoolyard favourite that's loved by everyone. It's a no-bake classic, though I've added some hazelnut meal and brandy to make it a little bit grown-up.

This crumble is flavoured with rhubarb, apple and dried figs, however the great thing about crumbles is they can easily be altered according to what's available. You could just as easily add frozen blueberries or raspberries to the apples, or combine pear and rhubarb. I've added almond meal to the crumble topping but this could be replaced with desiccated coconut or oats.

These biscuits can be served as a dessert with poached fruit and cream, or piled into a cookie jar for afternoon tea.

The Marsala mascarpone in this recipe is also beautiful served alongside any poached or baked fruit. The spiced biscotti is delicious as a simple dessert dipped into the mascarpone but there will also be enough left over to store in a jar and serve for afternoon tea.

ginger and lemon biscuits

MAKES APPROXIMATELY 35 BISCUITS

200 g (7 oz) plain (all-purpose) flour
½ teaspoon cream of tartar
½ teaspoon bicarbonate of soda (baking soda)
2 teaspoons ground ginger
½ teaspoon ground cinnamon
120 g (4¼ oz) soft butter
120 g (4¼ oz) caster (superfine) sugar
2 tablespoons golden syrup
1 teaspoon finely grated lemon zest
1 egg yolk

Preheat the oven to 170°C (325°F/Gas 3). Line two large baking trays with baking paper.

Sift the dry ingredients into a bowl and add a pinch of salt.

In a separate bowl, cream the butter and sugar until pale, then stir in the golden syrup, lemon zest and egg yolk. When combined, fold this mixture through the sifted dry ingredients.

Remove a heaped teaspoon of the dough, roll it into a ball and put it onto the lined baking tray. Lightly flatten it with your fingers. Repeat with the remaining mixture, allowing ample space between each of the biscuits for spreading. Bake for 10–12 minutes, until the biscuits are golden brown. Transfer to a wire rack and allow the biscuits to cool completely. Store in an airtight container until ready to serve.

spiced biscotti with marsala mascarpone

MAKES APPROXIMATELY 80 BISCUITS

300 g (10½ oz) plain (all-purpose) flour
220 g (7¾ oz/1 cup) caster (superfine) sugar, plus 1 tablespoon, extra
2 teaspoons baking powder
100 g (3½ oz) dried figs, sliced
50 g (1¾ oz) dried apricots, sliced
150 g (5½ oz) slivered almonds
2 teaspoons chopped lemon zest
¼ teaspoon ground cardamom
1 teaspoon ground cinnamon
3 eggs, whisked
200 g (7 oz) mascarpone
2 tablespoons sweet marsala

Preheat the oven to 180°C (350°F/Gas 4).

Mix the flour, sugar, baking powder, dried fruit, almonds, lemon zest, cardamom and cinnamon in a large bowl and make a well in the centre. Fold in the egg to make a sticky dough. Divide into four pieces and roll out each portion of dough to form logs 4 cm (1½ inches) in diameter.

Place the logs on a baking tray lined with baking paper, leaving space between each log to spread a little, and bake for 30 minutes.

Remove and allow to cool. Reduce the oven temperature to 140°C (275°F/Gas 1). With a sharp bread knife, cut each of the loaves into thin slices 5 mm (¼ inch) wide. Lay the biscuits on a baking tray and return them to the oven. Bake for 20 minutes, turning the biscuits once. Cool on wire racks.

Place the mascarpone, marsala and extra sugar in a small bowl and mix until smooth. Serve the biscotti accompanied with the marsala mascarpone.

blueberry slice

100 g (3½ oz/1 cup) pecan nuts
250 g (9 oz) caster (superfine) sugar
100 g (3½ oz) self-raising flour
grated zest of 1 lemon
150 g (5½ oz) butter, melted
4 egg whites
100 g (3½ oz/⅔ cup) frozen blueberries
245 g (9 oz/1 cup) crème fraîche
½ teaspoon natural vanilla extract

Preheat the oven to 150°C (300°F/Gas 2).

Grease a 18 x 28 cm (7 x 11 inch) or 22 cm (8½ inch) square baking tin and line it with baking paper.

Put the pecan nuts into a food processor and pulse several times to break into small pieces. Add the sugar, flour and lemon zest and process for 1 minute. Remove the dry ingredients to a bowl and stir the melted butter through.

Whisk the egg whites until soft peaks form, then fold them through the thick pecan batter. Pour the mixture into the prepared tin and scatter the blueberries over the top.

Bake for 25–30 minutes, rotating the tin after 15 minutes. Allow to cool in the tin.

Put the crème fraîche into a bowl and very gently fold the vanilla through. Cut the slice into rectangles or squares and serve with a dollop of vanilla crème fraîche.

This blueberry slice is flavoured with crushed pecan nuts, which bring a lovely caramel flavour to the cake as well as keeping it moist. You can serve it with the crème fraîche for afternoon tea or topped with a generous scoop of vanilla ice cream for dessert.

This is an old favourite. The texture is lovely and gooey and the flavour is zingy. When you make it the mixture will look as if it has split but it will all come good in the baking. Enjoy with a drizzle of cream or some ice cream.

lemon and coconut tart

SERVES 8

125 g (4½ oz) unsalted butter
345 g (12 oz) caster (superfine) sugar
4 large eggs
170 g (6 oz) plain yoghurt
1 teaspoon natural vanilla extract
3 tablespoons lemon juice
2 tablespoons finely grated lemon zest
90 g (3¼ oz/1 cup) shredded or desiccated coconut
1 pre-baked shortcrust tart case (see page 183)
icing (confectioners') sugar, for dusting
cream or ice cream, for serving

Preheat the oven to 180°C (350°F/Gas 4).

Beat the butter and sugar together until they are pale and creamy. Add the eggs one at a time and beat them into the mixture before adding the yoghurt, vanilla, lemon juice and lemon zest. Stir in the coconut and pour the mixture into the pre-baked tart case.

Bake for 30 minutes, or until the filling is golden and puffed. Dust with icing sugar and serve warm with cream or ice cream.

strawberry swirls

....

MAKES 20

250 g (9 oz/2 cups) plain (all-purpose) flour
½ teaspoon baking powder
110 g (3¾ oz/½ cup) caster (superfine) sugar
125 g (4½ oz) chopped unsalted butter
2 eggs, lightly whisked
115 g (4 oz/⅓ cup) strawberry jam
2 teaspoons ground cinnamon
icing (confectioners') sugar, for dusting

Sift the flour and baking powder into a large bowl, then add the caster sugar. Use your fingertips to rub in the butter until the mixture resembles coarse breadcrumbs. Slowly work in the egg until you have a stiff dough.

Roll out on a sheet of baking paper into a 20 x 30 cm (8 x 12 inch) rectangle. Spread the strawberry jam evenly over the dough and sprinkle with the cinnamon. Roll the dough up, Swiss-roll (jelly-roll) style, from the widest edge, peeling off the paper as you roll. Wrap in plastic wrap and refrigerate for 30 minutes.

Preheat the oven to 180°C (350°F/Gas 4) and line a baking tray with baking paper. Cut the roll into 1 cm (½ inch) slices. Put the rounds on the tray and bake for 15 minutes. Cool on wire racks and dust with icing sugar.

These biscuits were one of my grandmother's recipes. When we were young we went to her place each day after school. There would always be a jar of these in the kitchen to be enjoyed with a cup of tea. They've continued to be a favourite with everyone I've introduced them to.

I love a brownie but only if they are a bit gooey and not too sweet. This recipe ticks those boxes and is one of my favourites. I cut mine into little squares so I can justify going back for seconds, and occassionally thirds as well!

chocolate brownies

135 g (4¾ oz/1 cup) hazelnuts
330 g (11½ oz/1½ cups) sugar
4 eggs
55 g (2 oz/½ cup) unsweetened cocoa powder
85 g (3 oz/⅔ cup) self-raising flour
1 tablespoon natural vanilla extract
½ teaspoon salt
250 g (9 oz) butter, melted
100 g (3½ oz) dark chocolate, roughly chopped
100 g (3½ oz) white chocolate, roughly chopped

Preheat the oven to 175°C (335°F/Gas 3–4). Grease a 23 x 30 cm (9 x 12 in) baking tin and line it with baking paper.

Put the hazelnuts onto a separate baking tray and roast in the oven until golden brown. Remove from the oven and put the hazelnuts onto a clean tea towel (dish towel). Gather up the towel and rub the hazelnuts together to remove the outer husks. Discard the husks and roughly chop the hazelnuts.

Put the sugar and eggs into a large bowl and whisk with electric beaters until the mixture is pale and creamy. Add the cocoa powder, flour, vanilla and salt, and whisk to combine. Slowly add the butter and stir until all the ingredients are well combined. Stir the chopped chocolate and the chopped hazelnuts through the mix and pour into the prepared baking tin. Bake for 25–30 minutes.

Remove from the oven and allow to cool in the tin. Cut into small squares and store in an airtight container.

rhubarb sour cream cake

SERVES 10

3 tablespoons unsalted butter, softened
387 g (13 oz/1⅔ cups firmly packed) light brown sugar
2 eggs
1 teaspoon natural vanilla extract
300 g (10½ oz) sour cream
300 g (10½ oz) plain (all-purpose) flour, sifted
1 teaspoon bicarbonate of soda (baking soda)
1 teaspoon baking powder
400 g (14 oz/1 bunch) rhubarb, coarsely chopped
100 g (3½ oz) caster (superfine) sugar

Preheat the oven to 180°C (350°F/Gas 4). Grease and line a 25 cm (10 inch) spring-form cake tin.

Cream the butter and brown sugar using electric beaters, then add the eggs, vanilla and sour cream. Beat well, then sift in the flour, bicarbonate of soda and baking powder and fold together.

Spoon the batter into the prepared cake tin. Smooth the surface, then arrange the rhubarb over the top. Bake for 1½ hours, or until a skewer inserted into the centre of the cake comes out clean. If the cake looks like it is browning too quickly, cover with foil for the last 30 minutes. Remove the cake from the tin and allow to cool on a wire rack. When cool, lift the cake onto a serving plate.

Put the caster sugar in a small saucepan with 100 ml (3½ fl oz) water. Heat over medium heat until the sugar has melted, then increase the heat to high. Boil until the is starting to turn golden brown, occasionally swirling the pan, but not stirring the mixture. Quickly remove the toffee syrup from the heat and spoon over the rhubarb. Allow to cool before serving.

How gorgeous does this cake look? It's a real country-style one with lots of heart and soul. The toffee syrup that is drizzled over the cake at the end helps to balance the tartness of the rhubarb.

This is a lovely rich butter cake with an intense vanilla flavour. It can be served simply for afternoon tea or with cream and berries for dessert. I've baked it in a bundt tin because I love the shape but you can just as easily cook the cake in a basic ring tin.

vanilla and almond cake

SERVES 8–10

220 g (7¾ oz/1 cup) caster (superfine) sugar
200 g (7 oz/1¼ cups) blanched almonds
½ vanilla bean, finely chopped
250 g (9 oz) unsalted butter, softened
    and cut into cubes
4 eggs
100 g (3½ oz) plain (all-purpose) flour
2 teaspoons baking powder
mixed berries, to serve
icing (confectioners') sugar, to serve
thin (pouring/whipping) cream, whipped,
    or vanilla ice cream, to serve

Preheat the oven to 180°C (350°F/Gas 4). Generously grease a 27 cm (10¾ inch) bundt or ring tin.

Put the sugar and almonds in a food processor with the chopped vanilla bean. Process until the vanilla bean has completely broken down and the almonds look like coarse breadcrumbs. Add the butter and process until the mixture is soft and creamy, then add the eggs, flour and baking powder and process to a smooth batter.

Spoon the batter into the prepared cake tin and bake for 40 minutes, or until a skewer inserted into the centre of the cake comes out clean. If the cake is browning too quickly, cover it loosely with foil. Allow to cool in the tin.

Turn the cooled cake out onto a serving plate. Fill the centre with mixed berries and sprinkle with icing sugar. Serve with whipped cream or vanilla ice cream.

sultana cake

SERVES 10

385 g (13½ oz/2¼ cups) sultanas (golden raisins)
250 ml (9 fl oz/1 cup) hot Earl Grey tea
2 tablespoons brandy
350 g (12 oz) caster (superfine) sugar
250 g (9 oz) unsalted butter, softened
3 eggs, lightly whisked
310 g (11 oz/2½ cups) plain (all-purpose) flour
3½ teaspoons baking powder
½ teaspoon salt
100 g (3½ oz) blanched or flaked almonds

Preheat the oven to 180°C (350°F/Gas 4). Grease the base of a 20 cm (8 inch) spring-form cake tin. Line the side of the tin with a strip of baking paper that is 1.5 times the height of the tin. This will protect the cake as it rises.

Put the sultanas in a bowl and cover with the hot tea and the brandy. Allow to sit for 5 minutes.

Cream the sugar and butter using electric beaters, then fold in the egg. Add the hot sultana mixture and stir to combine. Sift in the flour, baking powder and salt and lightly stir to combine.

Spoon the batter into the prepared tin and arrange the almonds over the top. Bake for 1½ hours, or until a skewer inserted into the centre of the cake comes out clean. If the cake looks like it is browning too quickly, cover it loosely with foil. Remove from the tin and allow to cool on a wire rack.

chocolate mousse cake

SERVES 10

400 g (14 oz) dark eating chocolate
170 ml (5½ fl oz/⅔ cup) thin (pouring/whipping) cream
3 tablespoons Grand Marnier
6 eggs, separated
¼ teaspoon ground cinnamon
100 g (3½ oz/½ cup, lightly packed) light brown sugar
unsweetened cocoa powder, to dust
thick (double/heavy) cream or vanilla ice cream, to serve

Preheat the oven to 150°C (300°F/Gas 2). Grease and line a 23 cm (9 inch) spring-form cake tin with baking paper.

Put the chocolate and cream in a small heatproof bowl over a saucepan of simmering water, ensuring the base of the bowl does not touch the water. When the chocolate has melted, remove from the heat and stir in the Grand Marnier.

Beat the egg whites using electric beaters until stiff peaks form. In a separate bowl, beat the egg yolks, cinnamon and sugar until thick and fluffy. Fold the melted chocolate through the egg yolk mixture, then fold in the beaten egg white. Pour the batter into the prepared tin and bake for 45–50 minutes, or until a skewer inserted into the centre of the cake has some moist, but not wet, mixture on it.

Allow the cake to cool in the tin overnight. Just before serving, turn out onto a serving plate and dust with cocoa powder. Serve a thin wedge with a dollop of cream or vanilla ice cream.

I've talked about my grandfather and grandmother in this book, both of whom were important to me. My grandmother was on my mother's side and my grandfather on my father's side. It was my grandfather who had a sweet tooth and was forever baking cakes and biscuits. The kitchen had high cupboards and on top was an assortment of cake tins that were always eagerly opened to reveal each week's selection. His Anzac biscuits were always awarded points for crispness and this sultana cake was one of his favourites.

I think you have to end a book with a chocolate cake, as they are somewhat celebratory and, in the end, everyone's favourite. This one is flavoured with Grand Marnier and cinnamon and needs a dollop of cream or ice cream with it. For extravagance, add fresh raspberries.

INDEX

About the author

Michele Cranston has been cooking and styling food for more than twenty years, in a career that has included working as a chef in various restaurants, setting up an acclaimed cafe, cooking creatively for a food production company in London and writing about food. Michele originally trained as a visual artist but her love of food soon took her to the world of restaurants and food media. She has ten *marie claire* cookbooks under her wing. Michele's unique style demonstrates a love of fresh, clean flavours, crisp textures and a strong sense of colour and design.

Acknowledgements

This book may be a compilation of many books but there are still a lot of people to thank for taking it from an idea into a reality.

It started life as a concept discussed around a table with Amanda Maclean and Deb Brash, so thankyou both for giving me the opportunity to run with the idea. As always the Murdoch team have been fantastic and I thank everyone who has been involved in the process. In particular, I need to thank my publisher Anneka Manning, the designer Miriam Steenhauer who coped with far too many images, Lucy Turnow-West, the copy editor who asked lots of questions and Kit Carstairs, the project editor who ticked all the boxes and made sure I did everything. Thanks also to Alexandra Gonzalez who was in charge of Production and Pam Dunne who did all the proof reading.

Ultimately this is a book that celebrates my collaboration with a team of incredibly talented people over 10 years. So I need to also thank the previous teams at Murdoch who have worked on the books; the home economists who have tested the recipes and asked questions when necessary, the editors who have asked even more questions, the designers who have turned the photos and words into a beautiful book and the publishing and marketing teams.

Outside of Murdoch, I've had the great pleasure and honour of working with the very talented photographers who have been responsible for all these beautiful images and so I send an enormous thank-you to Petrina, Mikkel and Gorta. A big thank-you also goes to Christine and Margot, the stylists who have waved a magic wand over the food. The studio becomes a second home when we are shooting these books. And lastly, I must thank all the good friends who have helped me in the kitchen — I send a very, very big thankyou to Ross, Cathy and Heidi.

Last but by no means least, I send a heartfelt thank you to my family who raised me to think that anything was possible.

Thank you.

Published in 2012 by Murdoch Books Pty Limited

Murdoch Books Australia
Pier 8/9
23 Hickson Road
Millers Point NSW 2000
Phone: +61 (0) 2 8220 2000
Fax: +61 (0) 2 8220 2558
www.murdochbooks.com.au
info@murdochbooks.com.au

Murdoch Books UK Limited
Erico House, 6th Floor
93–99 Upper Richmond Road
Putney, London SW15 2TG
Phone: +44 (0) 20 8785 5995
Fax: +44 (0) 20 8785 5985
www.murdochbooks.co.uk
info@murdochbooks.co.uk

For Corporate Orders & Custom Publishing contact Noel Hammond,
National Business Development Manager Murdoch Books Australia

Publisher: Anneka Manning
Designer: Miriam Steenhauer
Photographer: Gorta Yuuki,
Mikkel Vang and Petrina Tinslay
Project Editor: Kit Carstairs
Editor: Lucy Turnow-West
Production: Alexandra Gonzalez, Karen Small

Text © Michele Cranston 2012
The moral right of the author has been asserted.
Design © Murdoch Books Pty Limited 2012
Photography © Anthony Ong, Gorta Yuuki, Mikkel Vang
and Petrina Tinslay

A cataloguing-in-publication entry is available from the catalogue
of the National Library of Australia at www.nla.gov.au.

A catalogue record for this book is available from the British Library.

Printed by 1010 Printing International Limited, China, Reprinted 2012

IMPORTANT: Those who might be at risk from the effects of salmonella poisoning
(the elderly, pregnant women, young children and those suffering from immune deficiency
diseases) should consult their doctor with any concerns about eating raw eggs.

OVEN GUIDE: You may find cooking times vary depending on the oven you are using.
For fan-forced ovens, as a general rule, set the oven temperature to 20°C (35°F) lower than
indicated in the recipe.

We have used 20 ml (4 teaspoon) tablespoon measures. If you are using a 15 ml (3 teaspoon)
tablespoon add an extra teaspoon of the ingredient for each tablespoon specified.